PRAISE

Life is a journey and how we travel through it makes the difference between an exhausting journey and a pleasant one. Barbara Mudge reminds us in this book that how we view the twists and turns along the way have a profound impact on our joy. She reminds us that the challenges of life are opportunities to have our faith in the Lord strengthened and that the joys of life are opportunities to thank Him for His love.

Pastor Thomas Olney

Barbara has captured the sentiments, thoughts and concerns of a young person growing up. This is definitely a book that should be read by a mother and daughter together. Each chapter will stimulate personal discussions and develop a warm closeness between mother and daughter that will make growing up a more understandable and comfortable time.

Dr. Walter Bogumil

Everyday wisdom is simple truths, painfully learned and actually applied. Barbara has learned how to get up again whenever and however she falls. In her simple stories, plainly told, are invitations to learn from her experiences and to be encouraged by her resilience. Here are the basics for a good life.

Dr. Lex Baer, Pastor/Psychotherapist

WHAT
KIND OF

Apple

ARE YOU?

Emily,
God is good.
all the time.

Barbara Mudge

Phil 4: 6-9

WHAT KIND OF Apple ARE YOU?

Barbara Mudge

TATE PUBLISHING & Enterprises

Published by Tate Publishing & Enterprises, LLC
127 E. Trade Center Terrace | Mustang, Oklahoma 73064 USA
1.888.361.9473 | www.tatepublishing.com

Tate Publishing is committed to excellence in the publishing industry. The company reflects the philosophy established by the founders, based on Psalm 68:11,
"The Lord gave the word and great was the company of those who published it."

Book design copyright © 2009 by Tate Publishing, LLC. All rights reserved.
Cover design by Jonathan Lindsey
Interior design by Joey Garrett

Published in the United States of America

ISBN: 978-1-60696-037-0
1. Religion / Christian Life / Personal Growth
09.01.22

DEDICATION

To the Holy Spirit who inspired every word of this book;

To the memory of my father, John Senti, who loved me;

To my loving and caring mother, Ruth Iverson, whom I admire;

To my wonderful husband, Bill, for his patience and understanding;

To my beautiful children, Debbie and Sarah, who are my life;

To my wonderful stepchildren, Bill, John, and Mary Beth, who inspire me;

And to my eleven grandchildren who delight me.

With all my heart I dedicate this book to the Lord to use as He may.

TABLE OF CONTENTS

INTRODUCTION

My name is Barbara, but you can call me Cindy—short for Cinderella. Remember that story? Cindy would sit in her own little corner and dream. The woods and fields were my little corners. I loved to escape for hours and talk with the animals both real and imaginary. Nature was my closest friend.

I was born a healthy nine-pound little girl the summer of 1955 in the wonderful, small town of Norwich, New York. I was second born among three brothers. My parents operated a dairy farm about five miles from town. I loved wearing beautiful hand-me-down dresses and pretending to be a princess. The tomboy in me loved to play with all the elements of nature. Many times you could catch me sitting in a mud puddle with my pretty dress on.

At the age of two, I started having grand mal epileptic seizures. Many times I would awaken after I had a seizure and find myself on the ground. Doctors prescribed medication for me, but that didn't control the seizures. I am still not sure how I developed epilepsy. Around the age of two, I fell down the cement barn steps, and at the same time I had a slight case of polio.

In kindergarten my teacher set up a cot in the back

of the room just for me. We used it when I felt dizzy or when I fainted. It was very embarrassing. I knew I was different at that point. Nobody else in my school had what I had.

I remember having a cot in the back of the classroom until fourth grade. After fourth grade most of my seizures were at night. I didn't have many friends. I can't blame them. They were afraid of the seizures.

Nature became my best friend and my little corner. Nature never rejected me or called me names like my classmates and father did. I always wanted to make my dad proud of me. He seldom gave me any praise as a child. He called me stupid, idiot, and jerk. These words were so engrained into my thinking that I thought they were true until I was twenty-nine years old.

My mother was a very caring person. I remember seeing her face over my bed at night as I would waken between convulsions. She was good to my brothers and me. She spoiled us by cleaning our rooms and doing chores that we should have been doing. While my father worked two jobs, my mother raised us and helped operate our dairy farm.

I couldn't wait to leave home. I wanted to escape it and everyone who knew me as an epileptic. I wanted to start a new life. And so I did. I went to a local community college and received a two-year degree in business.

I met Bill Mudge in 1976 during my last year of college. He was a wonderful man who was ten years my senior and treated me like a lady. This kindness was new to me. When I found out he had three children, I should have run the other way. I also found out he was separated but not divorced. I decided to give him and his wife time to mend their marriage without me around. I traveled

1700 miles from New York State to Houston, Texas, and lived with my brother and my mother for a year. This was a good test of Bill's and my love. I flew back to New York State in 1977, and we married in June of 1978 after his divorce was complete.

I was an instant mother of three beautiful stepchildren. They were eight, seven, and four when we married. I had two daughters with Bill. By the time I was twenty-six years old, we had five children. Talk about growing up fast. Many of the stories in this book were inspired by these wonderful children.

In 1985 Bill, our two daughters, and I moved to Florida from New York State on a wing and a prayer. I started work at the minimum of $4.60 an hour in a temporary receptionist position at our local utility company. While going to college part-time for a period of fifteen years, I also worked in the positions of cashier, customer service representative, administrative assistant, payroll/benefits administrator, and director of human resources in that same company. I graduated at the age of fifty with a bachelor's degree in business administration from the University of Central Florida on May 5, 2006. I also published a column in our local newspaper for over six years. What a journey.

All the glory goes to our Lord, Jesus Christ. He gave me the courage and helped me defeat the spirits of rejection, depression, and low self-esteem to enable me to write this book.

DAD'S TRIBUTE

I wrote my dad's tribute in 1998. That year I experienced the worst time in my life. That also turned out to be the best time for my personal growth.

My dad had been living with our family off and on for seven years. In 1997, at the age of seventy-one, he became very sick. He battled with diabetes, high blood pressure, and congestive heart failure. In December of 1997, my husband and I had to start controlling and recording my dad's medications and food intake. He went into a diabetic coma in Houston, Texas, while visiting my oldest brother, Russell, and his loving family during the Thanksgiving and Christmas seasons in 1997. Dad arrived back at our home in Florida on December 28, 1997. He needed to be cared for around the clock and needed his diapers changed. What a shock and change in our living patterns for my husband and me.

Many trials followed, and on May 24, 1998, my dad went to be with the Lord. Before my father's death I had been reading a book that instructed children how to write their parents a tribute. The tributes were to be given to parents while they were still alive. I was in the process of writing a tribute for my father when he suddenly passed away.

One of the best support teams I had at the time besides the Lord and my family and church were the members of the Toastmasters club. A Toastmasters club develops skills in both communication and leadership. I joined in August of 1997. I wrote and memorized the following tribute to my father two days before his funeral in New York State. I recited the following tribute at my dad's funeral service.

The following is Dad's tribute:

•

Dad is home. That's what I would cry out at about 4:00 in the afternoon each day when Dad came home after driving the school bus. Mom had dinner ready. We ate early because Dad had to go to his second job at the Norwich Pharmaceutical Company after dinner. I was in bed before Dad came home from his second job. When the weekend arrived, Dad was ours but only after he finished the farm chores and the honey dos.

Dad always made time to play football, baseball, ping-pong, and other sports with his children. To this day when I hear the ping of a table tennis ball, I have to seek out the game and ask to play. By the way, I'm pretty good.

In the summertime our family swam in the lake, and in the winter we ice-skated on it. My dad was the best ice skater I knew. I took great pride in saying, "That's my dad out there on the ice," when someone would ask, "Who is that?" We only had Dad for a few hours a week, but those hours were precious.

When Dad was busy milking the cows, he would squirt some warm cows' milk into my mouth. It tasted horrible, but it made my dad smile. Dad let me jump down from the top floor of the barn through the chutes into the haystacks and into the grain bin. I wanted to be near Dad even when he was doing his chores.

Whatever Dad was doing, I always heard him singing. He had a song for everything. My favorite time of singing was after we took a hayride around the lake. It was at that time that we sang for hours around the bonfire at the lake and toasted marshmallows.

Some songs I will always cherish are "Paperdoll," "Edelweiss," "Oh Johnny," and the "Mockingbird Song." Dad yodeled during the "Mockingbird Song." I loved to hear him yodel. I closed my eyes and imagined I was in Switzerland. His voice reminded me of Frank Sinatra.

Dad loved to take rides around the lake in the canoe or rowboat. He would always point out the beauty of nature to his children and grandchildren. He loved God's masterpieces. Dad loved God's creation whether he was at the lake, at the ocean, in the woods, or at a state park.

In 1978 I married a wonderful man. I thought I didn't need my dad anymore. In November of 1991, when my husband fell twenty feet off a church roof and broke his neck, my dad came from New York State to help us. Dad took my husband to doctor appointments because I had to work. Dad also mowed the lawn and did many other chores around the house that my husband could no longer do. This time was when we all developed a special love for each other. My dad stayed with us for the next seven-plus years between his adventures around the United States in his car.

During those blessed seven years, Dad and I took bike rides together. One ride we took was twenty miles long. We stopped after ten miles and had lunch before returning home.

My dad and I also walked on the beach at night together many times. We were awestruck by the stars and the moon shining upon the waves. Memories are beautiful.

I will never forget the love Dad had for people. Almost every day Dad would meet someone new. Dad would return home and tell us about his new friends. He always carried a camera because he loved to take pictures of his new friends. He sometimes asked them for their mailing address and sent them a photo.

I never saw Dad without a pack of peppermint Lifesaver candies in his pants pocket. His children knew they could always get a mint from him. He had the best breath in town.

In his final months of life, I saw anguish in his eyes. He was not able to care for himself. He would even ask me, "Why am I so crippled?" My husband now helped Dad just as Dad had helped him in 1991. Dad and Bill became very close.

I loved to look into Dad's beautiful blue eyes. He had such puppy dog eyes. On the trip up to New York State from Florida a week before he died, Dad used those puppy dog eyes to muster an extra cinnamon roll at a restaurant. He knew, because he was diabetic, he shouldn't have it.

Yes, Dad's home at last, and now he must watch and wait for us to join him someday.

•

Tributes are words of honor to your parents. Most of us don't say these words except at funerals. I wrote my mother a tribute when I returned to Florida after my dad's funeral. I wanted to let her know how much I loved and appreciated her.

You don't have to have perfect parents to be able to write a tribute. A tribute should be about the positive attributes of your parent. There has to be something good you can say. Honor your parents in a tribute while they are still alive to appreciate it.

The tribute you just read was for the same father who called me stupid, idiot, and jerk. My father had positive traits along with the negative. When my father lived with my husband and me the last years of his life, he didn't call me one of those negative names. I finally stood up for myself and asked him not to talk that way in my home. I would not allow him to speak any negative words to our children either. Time does have a way of improving relationships when you are willing to endure and love regardless of a return on your investment.

An acronym for TRIBUTE:

T   ouched by the
R   ich life of your parent.
I   nclude only the
B   lessings and
U   nique qualities
T   hat you remember.
E   xpress only the positive.

I joined our local Toastmasters club in August of 1997. One month later, I was elected vice president of public relations for our club. I started writing advertisements for our club in our local newspaper in April of 1998. At that time, I was allowed a small section in our local newspaper to announce the club's place and time of our meeting. As time continued on, I became more and more creative in this small column. When I turned in my dad's tribute in June of 1998, the editor of our local newspaper called and asked me to bring in a picture of myself. He said he wanted to give me my own column in the newspaper. I was shocked at this offer. I rejoiced in the ability to reach and encourage more people. The following story was published on June 18, 1998.

RED LIGHTS ARE FOR RELAXING

In July of 1998, as I was returning home from a Bible study group, I was thinking about the Fourth of July. That was my next holiday off work. As I stopped at a red light, God inspired me to think about freedom. Suddenly I saw the red traffic light representing bondage or trials in our lives and the green light representing freedom.

When you stop at a red light, you know it will turn green. Life has many red lights. We need to keep in mind that the red lights will eventually turn to green and we will go through them. They can't last long. They would be holding up traffic or progress.

Sometimes traffic lights get caught and won't change to green. Do you know what I do in that situation? I look both ways and then go straight through the red light. Some trials in life seem to be stopping you from having your freedom. I suggest that you look both ways and then proceed. Don't get stuck.

I live close enough to the ocean in Florida that I am able to see the sunrise every morning at the beach. Sometimes the clouds are so abundant that they hide the sun and its glory. The sun is like freedom. Even if your life is full of problems, there is freedom waiting for you behind those problems. We must wait patiently and believe that the sun will appear.

Freedom was obtained for our nation after many battles. Your freedom as an individual is a daily battle in your mind. The box that controls the traffic light tells it when to change. Our minds control our very being and tell us when to react and when not to react.

We have been programmed from childhood to react certain ways to certain problems. We must reprogram our minds daily to avoid being stuck at a red light.

Trials and red lights are a time of renewal and observance. Think about it. When I stop at a red light, I instantly grab my coffee mug and take a sip or two while I relax at the wheel. I can observe the cars and people around me. Sometimes I catch myself hoping for a light in the distance to turn red so I can sip my coffee again while it is still hot.

Freedom (green light) is great, and I'll take that any day over bondage, but along with freedom come risks. Freedom also has opportunities for adventure.

When you haven't planned your time well, the red light becomes a hindrance. Hindrances are there to train you and make you aware of the rest of the world around you.

The only difference I can see between a red light and trials of bondage is that red lights come one by one and trials can come more than one at a time. Even if the red lights come one after another, you will eventually hit the country roads where there are no red lights. Everyone move to the country, right? No. No red lights are nice, but everyone must experience them in order to grow.

Next time you come to a red light, say a word of

thanks that you have time to relax. Then give thanks for the assurance that the red light will change to green.

An acronym for FREEDOM is:

F   ocus yourself daily and
R   est in the assurance that
E   very trial is for your
E   ducation and for your
D   eliverance to freedom.
O   pen to guidance remain, and
M   ighty in wisdom become.

DON'T GET STUCK IN THE SAND

As I watched the sunrise one morning at the beach, I noticed a picnic table that had drifted out to the area of the rising tide away from the safety of the concrete boardwalk where it belonged. It gradually was getting stuck in the sand. In time it might be pulled out to sea unless someone rescued it and returned it to its correct location.

Then I remembered when my children and I would stand in the sand at the beach and let the waves roll over our feet. The waves would push the sand over our feet gradually. If we stood there long enough, the sand would cover our feet and our ankles.

We assisted the sand in covering our feet by wiggling our feet back and forth in the sand and pushing down hard as we wiggled. You can picture that, can't you? How often have you tried burying your feet in the sand? I suppose many times. Now let me give you a different perspective.

How many of you enjoy getting stuck in your troubles and enjoy going even deeper by desiring to receive pity and attention? Before you answer that question, let me tell you I write from experience. I write not to condemn you but to encourage you and strengthen you.

Many of us do enjoy getting stuck in our self-pity. I

learned very early in my life how pity could work for me and used the caring heart of my mother to get attention. Sometimes I even went as far as to stage temper tantrums. It worked.

I wasn't getting enough positive attention for my good grades and achievements, so I turned to the negative side and attracted pity.

When I married, I found out that my partner was not as willing as my mom to join in my pity party. That was very hard on both of us. This continued for the first ten years of our marriage. I would even poke my husband in the ribs when he refused to stay up and argue with me. I wanted to be right so badly that I would stage a tantrum.

Can you believe an adult in her thirties staging a tantrum? When I was forty-two years old, I was just starting to discover who I was and what talents I had hidden. For too long I kept my feet in the sand. I was almost pulled out to sea. I have pulled my feet out, and I now enjoy the freedom of living.

Having pity parties is a very hard habit to break. It takes much prayer, self-talk, and self-encouragement to stay out of the sand. You can do it. I know you can.

I still sink in the sand a little bit, but I have trained my mind to step out as soon as possible to avoid the temptation of becoming comfortable again. I suggest that if you enjoy the sand, make sure it is the white sand of the beach, not the sand of self-pity.

An acronym for SAND is:

S   tuck momentarily.
A   llow your mind freedom.
N   ever get comfortable there because you
D   eserve the best that life has to offer you.

LET'S PLANT A GARDEN

If you have ever planted a garden, you know that planning has to be done before you sow the seeds. You must decide first of all what to plant. Then you must decide where to plant it and when to plant each different kind of vegetable. Each seed package has specific planting and sowing instructions. The instructions should be followed to produce the best harvest.

If you have never planted a garden, have you ever put together a puzzle? I'm talking about a puzzle of five hundred pieces or more, not the easy ones. It takes time and planning and much patience to construct a puzzle, doesn't it? Sometimes you may even want to give up when you can't find a certain piece. I usually try to find another piece that's easier and then go back and find the harder piece. How about you?

I always seem to be asking you questions. Without questions there can't be any answers. Like *Jeopardy*, the question is the right answer. I always loved to watch *Jeopardy* as a child and even now when I get the time. When I was young, I would be so proud of myself if I knew even one correct answer. If you answer the questions I ask and answer them truthfully, you are on your way to accomplishing your goals in life.

Has your garden ever been damaged or destroyed by unwelcome animals or pests before the rich harvest came? Have you ever taken time and effort to put together a puzzle, and all of a sudden, someone accidentally knocks your puzzle on the floor? Been there, done that. How do you feel when your kids rush in the house after school and track mud and dirt onto your clean floor you have tediously cleaned all day? It makes you want to scream, doesn't it?

All of those illustrations represent planning, energy, hope, time, and patience. The garden, the puzzle, and a clean home can also be damaged or destroyed in a brief moment of time. We have seen firsthand in Florida how hurricanes, tornadoes, floods, and fires can affect our homes and lives. We have no control in these matters. No amount of planning can stop these natural happenings, but there are some happenings in life we can control to a certain extent.

For all of you who have or who have had children, we know how the seeds we have planted can take a long time in harvesting. Sometimes we never see the harvest of seeds planted in our children. The easy part is planting and watering. The hardest part of being a parent is waiting for the harvest of thankfulness and gratitude. The next hardest part is the weeding. We try to keep all the bad experiences out of our children's lives, but as they grow older, it gets harder for you to weed around them.

Children in their adolescent years are surely puzzles to parents. When your child becomes an adolescent, you as a parent feel like you have almost completed your task of raising your child. Then all of a sudden your child decides to reorganize the pieces and test your patience and endurance. Will you as parents continue to finish the puzzle, or will you give up and put the pieces back in the box and deal with it another time when you feel better about the outcome? I have a suggestion. Give the puzzle to your child if the puzzle does get too hard to complete and if your child is old enough. You can continue to give your child guidance, but let them try to finish their puzzle of life. Many times it's the letting go that truly hurts. It takes more strength to let go than to begrudgingly hold on and make a mess of the puzzle.

Can I let you in on a secret? There are no perfect families. There are families who have positive-perspective thinking. That simply means that some families believe that all things work for good no matter what mess is made of the puzzle. You have to believe that all things do work for good to survive in any family. You need to look at the trials your family experiences as instruments of growth and learning and not as problems.

At one time or another, have you experienced the thanklessness of your family? You clean your home all day long only to have unaware family members tramp in dirt and be unconcerned about throwing shoes and clothes along a path to their bedrooms. We won't even talk about the bathroom after your child takes a shower. Why don't they understand? When they are children, we excuse it as youth, but as they get older, we start to wonder why they don't respect our home and pick up after themselves.

Our children don't give us praise and consideration for keeping the house clean. The praise and respect will come but not until the harvest is ready. The harvest can come at the age of eighteen, but it may not come until later years in their twenties, thirties, or even forties. Each child has its own growing rate, just as each vegetable you plant has its own harvest time. The only thing we can do is plant, water, weed, and wait. Oh, I almost forgot. The most important gift we can give our children is unconditional love. That love will help the seeds grow that you plant.

When your garden, your puzzle, or your home have been reorganized, just turn to positive thinking and believe that all things do work for good. Remember, situations or trials are temporary, but families are forever.

An acronym for GARDEN:

G   ive love to your children,
A   nd you will be
R   ewarded eventually.
D   esire to love them
E   ven when that love is
N   ot earned or deserved.

DO YOU HAVE THE QUALITIES OF A FIREFIGHTER?

This story was written during the terrible Florida wildfires of 1998. I saw such wonderful qualities in our firemen.

Florida had been on fire. Our heroes were the firefighters. Why? They fought to protect our homes and properties with all their might. Even within an inch of their lives. Would you fight that hard for something you believed in? Do you have the qualities of a firefighter? The three most noticeable qualities they had were determination, knowledge, and selflessness.

Firefighters were determined to fight the fires no matter how high, wide, and furious the fires became. Because of intense training and continued learning, they were knowledgeable of how to fight fires of all sizes. They were selfless and unconcerned about their own lives. They focused on saving others' lives and homes.

Are we like firefighters? I wasn't. Oh, I was determined but only for what I wanted and for my own profit. Am I touching some sore spots? It is time for those sores to heal, and it is time for you to change your negative thinking. Determine in your mind to fight the fires of your life each day. Determine to not let negative thinking take over and burn you down to nothing.

One of the fires of my life has been the fear of rejection. Some big fires have been lit with this fear. After I allow one spark of rejection to enter, it leads to more negative thoughts and so on and ultimately into depression.

Depression is like the fires in Florida. When the fire gets too big and furious, it is very hard to fight alone. Help may have to be called in for a short time to get the flames under control. I did seek some temporary help, and it did help me focus. I determined in my mind to fight the hot spots to avoid the possibility of a fire starting again.

Knowledge is the number two quality. It is not something that comes naturally. Firefighters go through intensive training over and over again. We have learned from experience that repetition helps anyone of any age learn anything. When I was learning sign language, I repeated and repeated it till I could remember it without looking in the book. I was determined to practice, so I could talk better with my deaf friends. I stood in front of a mirror and practiced signing. I also practiced with my two daughters who knew sign language.

A new world started opening up to me when I started reading again for the first time since high school and college. In college when I had to read a book for class, I always read the condensed version from the library because I didn't like reading. I was always proud of my daughters when they would bring home awards for reading books in elementary school. They were taught that reading is fundamental. Reading *is* fundamental. I knew that, but for years I had let my brain become weak. The brain is a muscle and should be exercised. Reading is the best exercise for the brain, and it's painless.

Modern technology has made it even easier for all of us. We can now buy books on CDs or DVDs. There should be no excuse not to exercise your brain. It requires a desire to obtain knowledge and a determination to begin. Start reading today, even if you read only three to five pages of a book each day. Once you read for twenty-eight days in a row, you will develop a habit that you will not want to stop.

The last quality is the quality of selflessness. Some good advice is to do unto others as you would have them do unto you. The firefighters did this day after day as they fought the fires. They even gambled with their own lives to serve us. Now that's selflessness. They have families and homes to go home to, but they considered others first. Do we do that?

In my life the negative thinking started turning positive when I determined not to let the fires of life consume me. I consumed knowledge and understanding through reading and listening, then I applied these new concepts to my life.

Fires will come into our lives and into our minds. We must exercise our minds into correct thinking to constantly be prepared to fight our fires. See what I mean by firefighter qualities? You should thank them and appreciate them even more now.

An acronym for FIRE:

F ight with determination and
I ncrease in knowledge by
R eading a little every day and
E ver desire to be selfless.

WHAT KIND OF APPLE ARE YOU?

Do you know what kind of apple you are like? Maybe you are like a Macintosh, a Red Delicious, or a Rome apple. I was a Macintosh, soft and easily bruised. In fact, in my developing years, I didn't understand why everyone didn't like me. By the way, my developing years lasted almost forty-two years.

Everyone likes apples, don't they? Whatever kind of apple you are, I can promise you this, not everybody is going to like you all the time. Some people will never like you. Personally, I don't like some apples. Some are too sour. Some are too hard. Some are too soft. Just as each apple has its qualities, each of you are also unique and have a special purpose and special qualities within.

In a time of a financial need, I baked and sold homemade apple pies. I used only Macintosh apples for baking these pies. No other apple would do for me. The Macintosh had qualities that I needed for that specific purpose. I made and sold three hundred pies in a three-month period. Not to brag, but I can peel an apple in about thirty seconds without looking. Sometimes I could peel it in one long strip.

When I was young, I thought that I could get everyone to like me. I believed that somehow or some way it had to be possible. Unfortunately it was mission impossible. Just as you can't mix Macintosh apples with Red Delicious and come out with a good apple pie, so some people just can't be mixed together. Some people you meet just won't blend with you. Their personalities and qualities are too different from your personality.

Till I was forty-two years old, I would do almost anything to please people. By pleasing people I felt I was pleasing myself. In fact, I did do some things I am now ashamed of, but that's the past. Let's leave it where it belongs. The only thing the past is good for is learning. The past is the core of the apple that belongs in the garbage.

Three things in my past gave me the misconception that everyone should like me. Those things were the relationship I desired to have with my dad, television shows with people living perfect lives, and my low self-esteem. Let me elaborate on each.

Ever since I can remember, I wanted my dad to love and respect me. I was twenty-nine years old before he said "I love you." I was thirty-seven years old before I finally felt respect and acceptance from my dad. I believe that desire to please my dad had a lot to do with the desire for everyone to like me.

Television and movies influenced my belief that everyone lives in a perfect fairy-tale world. I loved watching the happily-ever-after movies such as *The Sound of Music* and *The Wizard of Oz*. Some sitcoms on television now show a more realistic side of life. Unfortunately those programs show that it is okay to be sarcastic toward authority figures such as parents. Maybe that's why there are so many broken families now. That's another subject.

I never thought people should dislike other people. I believed that we should live in harmony all the time with everyone. God does desire that we love one another. The only perfect place will be in heaven when we leave this world. There are no perfect people. Even apples that look perfect have small pinhole blemishes.

Low self-esteem added to my need to be liked by everyone. "If you don't love yourself, how do you expect others to love you?" was a question my mother asked of me when I was in my twenties. Before I began to like myself, I was very defensive toward anyone who corrected me in any way. I would get upset and feel rejected whenever anyone suggested I did something wrong. I am still working on this.

Variety is the spice of life, and the world does need all the different kinds of apples. I'll settle for the Macintosh that I am. After forty-two years, I finally discovered it is okay to not be liked by everyone. I was finally on my way to finding my true destination in life.

You can seek your true destiny and usefulness in life. Begin by loving yourself. Without taking that first step, all other attempts are in vain. Stay around positive people and look in the mirror and tell yourself that you are a wonderful creation of God. Apples have no choice as to what they will become or how they will be used but you do. It all starts in your thinking.

Next time you make a homemade apple pie, think of how special and unique you are. Put a shine on yourself as you would an apple, and offer yourself as a gift to the world by loving yourself first.

An acronym for APPLE:

A   ppreciate the
P   recious gem you are, and
P   olish yourself daily by
L   ooking in the mirror and
E   arnestly loving yourself.

DO YOU COLLECT GREEN STAMPS?

Some of you should remember S&H green stamps. I remember my mother receiving those stamps every time she bought groceries. My mom put the stamps into books and collected the books until she had enough to redeem the item we needed. She would then go to the S&H redemption center. It was exciting to see my mom go in with books filled with free stamps and come out with something useful like a barbecue grill or blankets. Sometimes it took months to collect enough stamps for what we wished for.

When I was talking to my pastor one night, I mentioned S&H green stamps. A smile came across his face. He told me he still has a sleeping bag that his mom had redeemed with green stamps years ago. When I told my husband of this story about green stamps, he excitedly said, "The chess set I have my mom redeemed with S&H stamps."

Like all good things, it ended. The redemption centers closed, and the grocery stores stopped giving out green stamps. Mom now had some useless and unredeemable books of stamps. Some of you may remember when the grocery stores around your area gave out stamps. We would fill up cards to get free food, such as tuna fish, bread, and eggs. I would go up to the grocery checkout counter with fifty dollars worth of groceries. I gave the cashier stamp-filled cards and received double coupons off the bill. My bill would be twenty dollars or less for a week of groceries for a family of four.

The green stamps my mother collected and the stamps I collected to reduce our grocery bill served the same purpose. That purpose was to redeem something of value from something that was free. The above are all positive rewards of collecting stamps.

Now let's discuss negative stamp collecting. Each time you get upset toward your employer, your husband, your wife, or your child, you collect negative green stamps. You put them into books in your mind. Every wrong said or done to you or every expectation not fulfilled by that person becomes a negative stamp in your book for that person.

I had quite a collection of stamps against my husband. I would try to cash them in each time we would argue by saying, "Do you remember when you . . . ?" Funny thing is I never seemed to redeem anything positive from trying to cash the books in.

The truth is I never cashed the stamps in. I took them back time and time again. Time and time again, I would try to redeem myself with the stamps collected against my husband. It took over ten years of playing that game in my marriage to finally realize I was in a losing battle. I achieved nothing but anger within myself. I also damaged my husband's self-confidence, and I frustrated him to his limit of patience many times. Now that I like myself better, I don't have the desire or the need to be right all the time. I don't need to collect green stamps anymore. Do you?

I realize that many of you have grown up collecting stamps since you were children. Others of you have learned how to use stamp collecting as a defense. Well, whatever the situation may be, habits like this should be unlearned.

Don't keep collecting negative green stamps. There are no positive rewards for negative stamps. Throw away the stamps; the grocery stores have. Now it's your turn!

An acronym for GREEN STAMPS:

G   et
R   id of
E   xtra baggage and
E   ver stay
N   estled in
S   pecial love
T   hat is
A   lways willing to
M   ake the
P   ositive rule and
S   eeks peace not war.

EVERYONE NEEDS TIME ALONE

Have you ever wanted to just get away from your surroundings and environment for thirty minutes? Everyone needs to get away.

I remember the feeling I had the first time I could afford a body massage. The thirty-minute massage left me totally relaxed. The tranquility I felt after that massage I also feel when I make time to be alone each day.

It takes a sacrifice. Usually it's a sacrifice of sleep time. I try to get up early enough to go to the beach. I relax and enjoy the sunrise and meditate on my Lord and the many blessings poured forth from him each day.

In 1998 I had fewer trips to the ocean because my attentions were on my newborn grandson and my daughter. They were living with us for two to three months. I did find time one Sunday afternoon to go to the beach in the late afternoon. I was fortunate enough to find a parking space right in front, so I could watch the waves and enjoy God's creation.

After I parked and turned off my radio, I heard some loud noises coming from beside and in front of me. Three teenage boys were being very rude and profane to each other. I kept my windows closed at first, but it became too hot to keep them closed.

Those boys wanted my attention. I said a short prayer and waited patiently. Nothing happened to better the situation. I had a choice to make. I could stay at the beach and continue to ignore them, or I could find a more serene place. I chose to go to the river instead. That was a good choice.

Life is full of situations like the one with those three young men. I guess I could have gotten out of the car and scolded them. Truthfully, that probably wouldn't have worked. The three young men saw they were not affecting me, and they decided to leave just as I decided to leave.

When I was twelve years old, I made a wrong choice when I reacted to a negative situation. A young man named Charlie Brown liked me. To get my attention, he called me "dog face." I was devastated. The other kids, seeing my devastation, joined in the game and called me "dog face" too. That name didn't leave my mind until I graduated from high school. Even then it echoed in my mind until I was twenty-nine years old. The wrong choice was that I responded to Charlie Brown instead of ignoring him.

I do realize there are some situations you might be going through right now that you can't ignore. Your choice should be to react positively when darts are thrown. Discernment and understanding in each trial will help you conquer that trial with or without a spoken response.

When you experience a situation that is uncomfortable, you can either stand there a target for the darts or keep your mind on all things good and pure and continue moving. A moving target is much harder to hit.

I have one last thought. Thank the Lord for every

obstacle of learning that comes your way. I thanked him for those three rude young men at the beach. They allowed me to write this. All things do work for good.

An acronym for OBSTACLES:

O   nly a
B   rief
S   econd of
T   ime in
A   ll eternity.
C   ling to and
L   earn from
E   very trial, the
S   ecrets of life.

DO YOU NEED FRONT ROW SEATS?

This story came to me one Sunday morning while sitting and waiting for church to begin. We held church in a school cafeteria. Our pews were movable, folding tables. The first pew was only three feet away from the pulpit area. A woman sat down in front of that area just as the pastor was getting his notes ready. Our pastor saw the woman and jokingly said, "You can stay there if you don't mind getting wet." In other words, sitting close may have its drawbacks.

My mind immediately traveled to Sea World and the sight of the people in the front rows as Shamu the whale splashed water all over their dry clothes. Those people had been warned ahead of time about what would happen if they sat in the front rows. Children would coax their parents into sitting there for the thrill of getting wet. The parents wanted to please their children, so they conceded.

Now let me share some other consequences of desiring front row seats.

When I was a child, I had a driving need to be as good as my brother in everything. I wanted the front row seat with my parents, but he usually received the glory of the front row. I imitated my brother until I was nineteen years old. It was at that time that I found out desiring the front row could be hazardous. My brother told me he was no longer a virgin. I wanted to be like him. Unfortunately, desiring to be the same as my brother had terrible consequences.

When you go to a concert or a theater production, you desire a close seat, don't you? But if you sit too close in the movie theater, your neck can hurt by the end of the movie. If you are too close during a concert, the speakers may hurt your eardrums.

I remember the one and only time I flew first class on an airplane. A friend who wanted to see me paid for the flight. I hadn't seen him for many years. First class was really nice. It was great to feel important, but I hadn't realized that it had a price tag attached. I was just a shy nineteen-year-old farm girl from upstate New York in the big city of Houston, Texas. The male friend who flew me first class didn't want to be just my friend. I fly coach now, and I pay my own way. I have no problem taking a second row seat.

The Saturday my second grandson was born was another good example of front row seats. My husband, my daughter Debbie, and I arrived at the hospital about an hour and a half after my seventeen-year-old daughter, Sarah, had gone into labor. I was already exhausted from spending the day with my grandson, Ryan, and Debbie at the mall getting Ryan's first pictures taken. My daughter Sarah already had a good friend of hers coaching her and holding her hand. I wanted so badly to be able to coach her as I had done with her nineteen-year-old sister, Debbie, only three months prior. Unfortunately, when I asked Sarah, she said she wanted her friend to coach her. I was totally hurt and felt rejected. I had been kicked out of the front row. It was selfish of me to think only of my own feelings. It only took a brief moment of a pity party, and then I apologized to both my daughter and her friend. I had realized it would be better to sit in the second row than to be kicked out of the event.

I was able to watch Sarah's almost ten-pound boy, David, come into this world. Sarah's sister, Debbie, was able to be in the front row. I enjoyed the event just as much from the background.

Don't get me wrong. I'm not saying if you sit in the front row at church or Sea World or anywhere else that you are wrong. I'm simply saying that the overwhelming desire to be first can be met with consequences. It's okay to be in the background sometimes. Be happy whether you have front row seats or not.

An acronym for FRONT ROW:

F   orfeit the
R   ight to be first and be
O   pen to the
N   avigating of
T   he Lord, and
R   ich and
O   bvious will be the
W   inners in life.

DO YOU LIKE SLOW TRAINS?

One Saturday morning as I was on my way to watch the sunrise at the beach, I received a good lesson in patience.

I left my home at 5:50 a.m. First I stopped at the post office to drop off some letters. I then proceeded toward the credit union to get some money from my savings account. What I call my savings is more like an elevator. It goes up and then down. Anyway, I needed money to pay for an oil change in my car before heading up to New Jersey. My daughter and I were going to pick up my son-in-law from coast guard boot camp. Our car needed to be ready for the trip.

It was very dark at 6:00 a.m. when I traveled toward the credit union. As I approached the stop sign, I could see flashing lights at the railroad track. I knew from experience that the early morning trains could take a long time. I decided to wait because I only needed to travel two more blocks to reach the credit union.

There was one car on the other side of the tracks when I stopped for the train. Two more cars joined the procession on each side of the tracks. There are other crazy people who get up early on Saturday mornings.

At 6:15 a.m. two cars gave up and left. When their

lights flashed on the tracks, I saw that the caboose was sitting right smack in the middle of the track. I decided to wait. It couldn't be long now, right?

At 6:25 a.m. the last car waiting at the tracks decided to turn around and leave. I was tempted to leave, too, but that caboose had only a few feet to travel to end the train. Isn't it so true that we give up sometimes on the brink of a miracle?

The caboose started crawling like a snail just as I decided to turn my car off and lean my seat back. I became a winner at 6:30 a.m. and crossed the track without getting stressed out and without turning back.

I did get to the credit union. Then I stopped and bought a cappuccino and headed for the beach. I arrived in time to see the sunrise. All week the sun had risen at around 7:15 a.m., but today for some reason the sun rose at 7:35 a.m. It was a miracle.

The qualities needed to wait for the train to pass reminded me of the qualities needed in many situations of life. Some situations take too long to end. It takes time, patience, and hope to wait for trains.

Any situation of life that seems to linger can be stressful and discouraging. TTT (Things Take Time) was one of the acronyms I taught my children. When my children were impatient, I would say, "Remember, dear, TTT." My children would smile a half smile and then ask again in about five minutes. We are like children. We want things to happen in our time.

One night when I went to a surprise birthday party for a long-time friend of mine, I was reminded of the need to be able to wait. The party was held in her church, which was still under construction. Members of the church were everywhere working to finish the building. The pastor told me that their prayer was to finish it by November of that year.

When I asked the pastor what his original vision was for the church, he delighted me with his answer. He said his original vision was not a building but a group of members that would act and perform as a loving community of God. That vision has been achieved and the building will simply be an added bonus. How about you? What are your visions and goals? Are trains interfering with your plans? My goal and vision for my life now is to use my experiences of the past and present to encourage people to have hope in their future. All of us have talents and abilities that can help others.

Next time you come to a morning train situation, remember it takes time and patience and hope to cross that track.

An acronym for TRAINS:

T   emporary
R   estrictions
A   nd tests in life.
I   nterruptions but
N   ot an end to hope.
S   trive on.

BURNT MARSHMALLOWS

On Halloween, my husband and I attended a Harvest Hoe-Down at our pastor's house. We walked slowly up a long driveway to the pavilion area. Many smells and sights caught my attention. Brown paper bags lit by candles lined the walkway. The smell from a large pumpkin carved with the church's initials floated in the air. This all brought back memories of New York State and the farm that I grew up on. We were greeted by more nostalgia in the pavilion. Hay bales were everywhere along with pumpkins and gourds displayed by spotlights. There was even a hay bale maze for the children. The food tables were decorated with fall tablecloths, and candles and acorns were scattered on the tables.

I sat down after greeting several members dressed up in farmer attire. Even though people were hungry, they sat or stood patiently waiting for the pastor to offer a prayer for the food before starting. When we have no control over events, we simply have to be patient and wait.

All through the evening, I watched as people waited for the different events. Only a small group of members in charge of the events knew what was going to happen next. This didn't bother those people not in control.

They simply trusted and left the results of the night in the hands of a few.

As the night came to an end I ventured to the back of the pavilion where a pitted bonfire had stayed lit during the whole evening. I had been visiting the fire many times during the night for sentimental reasons.

Back on the farm in upstate New York our family would often take hayrides during the summer and fall seasons. We would ride on a big wagon around the manmade lake, up into the hayfields, and back. We then sat around a carefully prepared bonfire at the lake and sang for hours. My father was the music leader. He loved to sing. He taught me many old songs of the thirties, forties, and fifties.

As I walked to the table near the bonfire at my pastor's house, I noticed they were starting to toast marshmallows. This was the only event of the night where each person could make an individual decision. I saw different levels of patience. Some people burnt their marshmallows quickly to a crisp. Very few took time and patiently toasted their marshmallows to a perfect brown on all sides.

The gist of this story is that we usually take the quick-and-easy way. Next time you are at a bonfire try taking your time to brown your marshmallows; see the greater taste and satisfaction that comes from that kind of patience.

An acronym for PATIENCE:

P   ut in priority
A   ll that you thought
T   o be very
I   mportant needs, then
E   liminate those
N   ot necessary and
C   arry out the rest
E   ver so patiently.

KEEPING UP WITH THE JONESES

Every year around November, people start talking about what they will buy everyone for Christmas.

I personally dread the season to be jolly. In fact, sometimes I become depressed and pray that Christmas will come and go as soon as possible. November and December for many years have brought not only health problems for our family but financial problems as well.

Every year, without exception, something major breaks down. One year it was the septic tank. We had to put in a new mound septic system. The next year, I ended up in the hospital, and then my husband broke his neck. The next year my husband had a kidney operation. You get the idea.

Maybe it's a fear of not being able to keep up with the Joneses that depresses me. I have always wanted to buy my children lots of gifts for Christmas, but we were unable to do that. With five children and many grand-children, it can get expensive even if only ten to twenty dollars per person is spent.

I have a wonderful friend who taught me the impor-tance of giving. Years ago when I first moved to Florida, we went around to garage sale after garage sale together. I would watch her buy things not only for her family but also for others whose needs she knew. She gave and gave. She even worked as the director of the homeless shelter without pay.

One Christmas my children did receive everything they wanted. How? My husband had fallen and broken his neck in November of 1991, and in December, a group of students from New Smyrna Beach High School brought Christmas to our home. What a blessing. Most of the things my girls wanted and received became unimportant about two to three months later. Even the permanents put in their hair were disliked in a few months.

I'll never forget the desire of my one daughter to have a Billabong jacket when they were in style. I made an agreement with her. If she could earn half of the money, I would pay the rest. She was only in fifth grade, but she did get the money. It took her six months. I was ready to follow through with my part of the bargain. She then told me that she didn't want to buy that jacket anymore.

My youngest daughter was crazy about the New Kids on the Block when she was eight years old. She wanted to have their tapes and anything associated with them. I told her to wait about six months. Then I asked her if she had ever heard of Three Dog Night. She said, "The what?" I said, "Case closed." My daughter now snickers when I mention her desires of the past.

People that try to keep up with the Joneses are like people waiting for tomorrow. They will never be satisfied. Tomorrow never does come. When you think tomorrow has come, it becomes today again.

When each Christmas season approaches, I pray that you as well as I can learn to accept our purchasing capabilities and be content. Remember the real reason for the season. Let's forget about keeping up with the Joneses and enjoy the gift God has given us.

Have the attitude of the apostle Paul. He was bound in chains in a cold prison cell, yet he was thankful and content in whatever position of life God allowed him to be in. Contentment is the word you and I need to keep in mind during the Christmas season and all year round.

By the way, my husband miraculously went back to work three months after breaking his neck. Doctors couldn't understand why he wasn't paralyzed or dead from his fall. Praise the Lord.

An acronym for CONTENT:

C   herish the small things and
O   penly thank God every day.
N   eed for nothing, but
T   rust that each and
E   very need will be met.
N   ever forget
T   hat you are loved.

365 DAYS OF LOVE

I remember a children's Christmas play my stepsons participated in years ago when they were only seven and eight years old. The play was called 365 *Days of Christmas*. The main song had these words in it: "365 days of Christmas each year. Every day's a day to smile, for God's love shines all the while." Every day is a day for God's love to shine through us. In May of 1998 when our family started experiencing divisions, we sought counseling. We counseled for almost two months. The counselor made a suggestion to me to start a journal. He suggested writing down everything that happened to me day after day. He also suggested writing what I did for other people day after day. Journaling helped me realize that I had been a blessing to others and that I do have worth in this world.

God showed the gift of love in the birth of his Son. Do you think that you can show love like that all year? I don't mean gift giving in a material sense. I am talking about the priceless, free gifts of time, understanding, love, and communication.

Don't let your feelings and emotions operate your life. That will get you nowhere fast. An engine of a train represents the facts. The middle car is faith. The caboose is your feelings and emotions. The caboose has no power and can't move without the engine. The facts we need to be empowered by are: God loves us unconditionally, so we must love everyone the same way or lose our power to move forward.

The feelings of rejection, anger, and worthlessness entered my mind too many times the year of 1998. In June I finally realized I was trying to move the caboose without an engine. Since I was going nowhere with my emotions, I started becoming the engine. I believe my emotions made me selfish.

A great part of my healing started with a story I wrote in June of 1998. It was the tribute I wrote for my father, who passed away May of that year. Writing has been very healing for me. The year of 1998 could have been the worst year in my life, but it turned out to be the best one. I became a mother-in-law and a grandmother twice, developed a special love for my now deceased father, and became a speaker and a writer. My two daughters and my father all left our home that year. What a year.

I challenge each one of you reading this story to desire to live 365 days of love and to be empowered by the engine and not by the caboose.

An acronym for "LOVE"

L   et the engine
O   perate your life.
V   ictory is in giving.
E   very day be a blessing.

THOUGHTS AND WHISPERS JUST WON'T DO

Years ago when I taught a fifth and sixth grade Sunday school class, I tested an exercise from one of the manuals. It suggested greeting each student as they entered the classroom. It also suggested giving each one of them a small gift such as a candy bar. The lesson that day was about giving thanks. As I greeted the children and gave them a candy bar, I counted how many children actually took the time to say thank you. Would you believe out of twelve students only four said thank you? I'm sure their parents taught them proper manners, but society teaches them differently. Society teaches them and us that the giver should know that the receiver is thankful without words.

How many wives would faint if their husband said something such as "Dear, I really appreciate the way you keep the house clean" or "Thank you for taking care of our children so well"? Too many times wives fall into the depressive state of mind with thinking such things as *Who really cares anyway?* or *Everyone takes me for granted.* Nobody is coming to your pity party, so stop it before it starts. True, men don't always say what we want to hear or when we want to hear it.

After reading Evelyn Christiansen's book *Lord, Change Me,* I began to change my way of thinking and speaking. My first reaction to that book was, "Who, me? I don't need to change; he does." Then I let go of my selfish desires and let humility sink in. As I began to compliment my husband and pray for him, he began to do the same for me.

My husband now makes me feel very special. He opens the car door for me almost every time if I don't forget and do it myself. He treats me like a lady and not a possession. That took years of patience and self-surrender. Did you notice I said self-surrender? I would wait as he walked to my door after he forgot to open it for me. I never said anything negative. I just smiled and verbally told him how honored I felt when he did those things for me.

I taught both of my daughters at a young age to expect these courtesies from any male friend they encountered. In fact, that's how my daughters weighed their relationships many times. I have to say that both of my sons-in-law are very good to my daughters in that respect. I can see also that both husbands are honored and thankful to have such precious jewels for their wives. That's how mates should feel about each other.

You men who are reading this, I'm not throwing all the weight of responsibility on your shoulders. Women must honor you and treat you with as much respect as you do them. The difference is the Bible says you men are head of the house. That does leave most of the burden on you to produce a thankful atmosphere in your home.

I have one more word for you, men. Don't judge your progress in this pursuit of excellence by the chemical imbalance of your wife that happens once a month. I, personally, would actually come home the day my imbalance started and warn both my children and my husband that there was a lion in their house for a few days. They usually reacted accordingly and avoided me like the plague if they were smart. Fortunately, time and vitamin B complex have helped tame my lion and left her almost toothless.

I did it again. I sidetracked from the thought of being thankful. Or did I? After all, to honor and respect your mate simply means to be eternally thankful for him or her. The real difference is verbally expressing that thankfulness or not. Even God spoke the world into existence. He didn't think it or whisper it. He spoke it.

Another book I read over twenty years ago still impacts my life today. That book was Charles Capps' *The Tongue, the Creative Force.* I had heard the destructive tongue from my father. This book was a brand new idea to me. What could I lose by trying? I began speaking positive words. Over much time, it became an excellent and uplifting habit. Not only did I start seeing the positive in others, but I also spoke positively to them no matter what negatives I might also see in them. People respond to positive words.

Our anger, judgmental attitude, and self-pity must leave us to truly love one another as God loves us. Thank God for the blessings he has given you. Too many of us say thank you only after opening a present.

I suggest that each morning as we roll out of bed we should thank God for yet another day to encourage others. God will bless you in abundance. I promise.

An acronym for THANKS:

T   enderly give words that
H   old only love and that
A   llow positive growth.
N   ourish those you love with
K   indness not only in works but
S   poken aloud daily.

DO YOU HAVE A NORMAN ROCKWELL LIFE

Is your life more like a Norman Rockwell painting or a *Saving Private Ryan* film? Let me explain my analogy. Norman Rockwell paintings are beautiful, still illustrations of perfect lives. I love these paintings because they are peaceful and they never change. Unfortunately, they are not realistic of life.

When I was a teenager, my family went on a short trip to Pennsylvania through Amish country. I marveled at the simple, pure lifestyle the Amish portrayed. I watched their horse-drawn buggies as they traveled through the covered bridges. I wondered if life was as perfect in their homes as it seemed to me on the outside. I will never know that answer, but I bet you that their families have problems too. No family, not even an Amish family, is a perfect Norman Rockwell family.

When the movie *Saving Private Ryan* came out in the theater, I debated whether to see it or not. I had heard of how realistic this film was. I did see it, and I'm glad I did. War is real. Life is real. Our lives are all real like Private Ryan's. Our lives are all affected by bombs either thrown directly at us or buried somewhere ready for us to step on. In more than one way, our lives must have strategies and battle plans to avoid death. We must learn to help each other as troops help one another. You too are a soldier in the film of life. I start each day with armor to protect me so I can combat the daily battles of life. That armor is found in Ephesians 6:10–18. The most valuable part of armor to me is the helmet. My mind is where most of my battles are won or lost. If I allow my mind to think negative thoughts and attitudes, I can lose the battle. A negative thought is like yeast. Just a little bit can expand 'til it fills your entire mind.

When I think of peacefulness and contentment, I think of our beautiful lake in upstate New York. I remember being awestruck when the lake would turn into a giant mirror. I could stand at the shoreline and bend over to see my reflection. The water was so still, yet I discovered that under the waters there were battles. Algae would fill up the lake once a year. I was astonished when my mother told me the lake was cleaning itself when it looked the ugliest. Even your messiest battles can work for good.

No matter how "Norman Rockwell" a family looks to you, there are some "Private Ryan" battles taking place there. There is motion below their still waters. Put on your full armor every day before you go into battle, and you will not only save yourself, you will save your family too. So pray up and suit up every morning. We can all be victorious.

An acronym for REAL:

R	ich in learning
E	very day should be.
A	llow the battles to
L	ift you to victory.

DUST OFF YOUR SPICES AND
ADD FLAVOR TO YOUR LIFE

My husband is very creative in the kitchen. He loves to cook and experiment with different spices in different recipes. Most of the times it turns out delicious, but once in a great while, I don't like the recipe. I venture sometimes and prepare different recipes from the cookbooks that are gathering dust in the bookcase. You have some gathering dust too, don't you? Well, it's time to dust them off and be adventurous in life.

The following story came to me when I was preparing my usual breakfast on the stove at 6:00 in the morning. As I was beating my egg and milk together with a fork, my eyes saw the spice rack next to the stove and its wide variety of spices. God whispered to me, "My people are like spices. Each one is unique and useful." I agreed with him.

Have you ever gone to the mall to just sit and watch people? My dad used to do that at malls and parks. He would inevitably introduce himself to one or two people as they sat down beside him on the bench. As I was growing up, my dad was prejudice. In his later years, it

Barbara Mudge

didn't seem to matter what color or nationality a person was. That's the way it should be for all of us.

People and their cultures and personalities are as different as the spices on your spice rack. I had some spices I had never attempted to use. I was afraid to use them because I didn't understand how to use them. I thought I might fail in the kitchen if I tried. It is just that attitude that makes us afraid of certain people. We worry that they won't like us or that they would add nothing to our lives. I was wrong, and so are you, if we fear these things.

All spices have a purpose and should be used and enjoyed. All people are special and should be enjoyed and savored. There isn't anyone that should be left on the rack.

God made a variety of animals and plants. Not just a few. He also made people diverse and wonderfully different. I still wonder why God created cockroaches and poison ivy. Why would God make those little sugar ants that no one seems to be able to get rid of? I'll know those answers someday, and so will you.

I always enjoyed learning foreign languages. I may not be able to talk very long with a Norwegian, a Greek, a Chinese, a German, or a Frenchman, but I can show them I care enough by saying "hello" and "how are you" in their languages. They are pleasantly surprised when they hear their own language. I can speak to my deaf friends fairly well. I'm not trying to turn you all into linguists. Expand your spice rack beyond America and beyond your own kitchen and comfort zone.

Next time you sit in the mall waiting for your spouse or teenage children to spend your hard-earned money, observe the variety of people that God has put in your

70

path and try to create a recipe. If someone sits near you, dare to introduce yourself. You may be the only person they talk to that day. I still remember the words to the Beatles' song "Eleanore Rigby," "I look at all the lonely people." You may be looking at a lonely person. Dare to communicate. You may be the spice today for that person's life. Don't be afraid to come off the shelf. Blessings are waiting for you and for others.

An acronym for SPICES:

S pecial are the
P eople you chose to
I nclude in your
C ircle of life.
E ver seek to
S avor the moments.

PIT STOPS ARE FOR REPLENISHMENT

Sunday afternoons are wonderful times to rest and retreat for a while. One Sunday after church, my husband and I went out to lunch. When we came home, we both took a nap. I take shorter naps than my husband, so when I woke up, I decided to go to the river and write this story.

I stopped at the gas station for my usual cup of cappuccino. It gives me extra inspiration. I have gained ten pounds since I became addicted to cappuccino.

As I was coming back to the car with my cappuccino, I saw a mother and her young son. She had just filled the tires on his bicycle with air. She was helping him travel the short distance on his bike to their car in the parking lot. They almost reached the car safely when I overheard her say to her son, "I know you can do it next time." I could tell that the training wheels had been removed recently and the young boy was now trying to ride on two wheels instead of four.

I bet his mother had given him that same encouragement many times before. We have a parent that will never give up on us and will encourage us every day. No matter how many times we fail, our Father will be there to pick us up and say, "I know you can do it next time."

Toward the end of Tuesday night Bible study group, one of the women prayed a beautiful prayer asking the Lord to help us out of our pits. As my eyes were shut, I envisioned the Daytona racetrack and the many pit stops the drivers have to make during each race. When the prayer concluded, I shared with the ladies in the group what I saw.

God showed me in this illustration how we can be helped during the pit stops of life. At pit stops, drivers receive repairs on their cars and get replenished, so they can continue in the race. If a driver doesn't stop for a pit stop, he will not finish the race. He will probably break down.

Everyone goes through pits once in awhile. The important thing to keep in mind is that pit stops are fast and are over within a short while. *Yeah right*, you say. Your pit stop may seem to last too long, but in the race of life, your pit stop is only a blink of an eye.

God allows people to help you get out of the pits and back into the race. Don't give up on yourself and don't stop in the middle of the race. There are three differences between the racecar driver and yourself. The driver knows how long the race is going to be, he knows where the pit stops are, and he gets to pick his own pit crew.

A good way to be sure you will always have a pit crew of your own is to be a part of other pit crews. Give and it shall be given. If you continue to be a pit crewmember, you will never have to worry about who will help you during your pit stops.

After I bought my cappuccino, I headed for the river. Believe it or not, there they were again. The mother and her son were there at the park. She was still supporting him as he attempted to ride the bike alone. I don't know if the son succeeded that day without his mother's help, but I am positive he will someday.

Of my children, only one never needed training wheels. That was my stepdaughter, Mary Beth. When she was just five-years-old, she insisted she wanted to ride her big brother's bike. That bike was almost too high for me to ride, but upon her insistence, we put her up on the seat. To our surprise, Mary Beth rode that two-wheel bike on her first try. She did need help getting off the bike. Even when Mary Beth became pregnant at fifteen years old, she wore a confidence. She is now a great mother of five children and is still as confident and sweet as when she was five-years-old.

Some people have natural confidence like Mary Beth, but others have to develop that confidence gradually. If you still need training wheels, that's okay. There's no shame in that. I had training wheels until I was twenty-nine years old. It was at that time that I was healed of epilepsy. I came off medication I had been taking for twenty-seven years.

An acronym for PIT STOPS:

P   ush on and
I   n all
T   rials of life.

S   eek always
T   o see
O   nly the good.
P   it stops are to be
S   avored and enjoyed.

CHOOSE YOUR BLACKBERRIES CAREFULLY

Every time I attempt to write a story, I ask the Lord for a vision. For this story, he gave me a vision of myself picking blackberries. I loved to pick blackberries, strawberries, raspberries, and black caps when I was young.

I would plan the day ahead of time and wait one to two days after it had rained. That allowed the rain to soak into the blackberry bushes and the sun to ripen them to perfection. I started early in the morning to avoid the hot sun during the day. Blackberries blossom in the month of August. That's the hottest month— sometimes the only hot month—we had. When it hit the eighties there, it was as hot as when it hits the hundreds here in Florida.

It was necessary to dress up like winter. I put on old jeans and an old long-sleeved shirt to protect myself from the briers. From our farmhouse, I walked across the hayfield to the twenty-two-acre manmade lake. I then proceeded across the dike at the south end of the lake and up the steep hill to the west. There at the top were bushes and bushes of berries. Some bushes were taller than I was.

With my empty cutout milk jugs in my hands, my mission was clear. I would pick until I filled the jugs, no matter how long it would take.

Getting to the bushes was the easy part. Now it was time for the test of patience. I think I have super sonic eyes because I could see the biggest and ripest berries from yards away even through the thick briers.

I proceeded to knock down the bushes by kicking them with my legs in wide sweeps. Can't you just picture me fighting the briers down to get to the best berries? I was only nine years old, standing at a whopping four foot, when I first attempted this. There were many smaller unripe berries that would have been much easier and quicker to pick, but I only wanted the best. That meant more time and energy.

I wanted only the ripest and juiciest blackberries. The ones that explode with juice on your fingers as you pick them. The ones that are so sweet you don't need to add any sugar to your pies. They are worth fighting past the sour ones, and they are worth the concentrated effort it takes to pick them.

Each one of us is sinless every day. We don't say a harsh or nasty word to anybody. Then we decide to get out of bed. That's when rather than *being* sleeping angels, we *need* angels. Being human, we have emotions and feelings. Some emotions produce unripe berries and make your life sour. You need to kick down those emotions and look for the more perfect berries.

The blackberries represent the words that you speak daily. Take your time and choose the best words. Don't settle for the sour words that emotions can bring out. Nobody likes sour blackberry pies. If your words are ripe and well chosen, your pie in life will be too. People will want to listen and taste the purity and wisdom of your words.

In order to have blackberry pie in the winter, I would freeze some berries. May I suggest that you make a habit of freezing some good words in your mind? Frozen foods are just as good and tasteful as fresh picked.

Remember that words once spoken are like berries once picked. They can't return to their source. They have been set loose. The person receiving these will either joyfully digest them or spit them out in distaste.

I can remember one time I had an encounter with my second oldest stepson, John. He was fourteen years old at the time and very independent. He was and is a person who speaks his mind. One day after I returned from a long day of work, John loudly started complaining about the house rules. After about two to three minutes of letting him speak, I asked him if I could take a time out to go to my bedroom. I knew if I stayed I would have picked some sour berries. In my room, I prayed to the Lord to fill my mouth with his words for John. I had gone berry picking. I then returned to John and in love expressed myself. God is so good. God not only filled my mouth with good words, but he gave me love for John despite his attitude toward me. We talked calmly and came to an understanding.

You don't always have time to take a time out, but we can have some good berries in the freezer section of our minds. Love bears all things and endures all things. Love is the only fruit that will never end. Next time you pick berries or eat a berry pie, think about the sweetness of the berries and the time and effort it took to pick them.

An acronym for CHOOSE:

C   are enough to
H   arvest lovingly
O   nly the best and
O   mit the bad berries.
S   pecial are words
E   arnestly picked.

QUALITIES OF MY DOG

He was a white, ten-year-old French toy poodle. Because of his age, he had become blind in one eye. God showed me a quality in my dog that all of us should strive to achicve.

Maurice was a persistent beggar. When I ate something in the living room, he would sit and look at me with loving eyes. Those eyes seemed to say, "Please, please." If I didn't respond, he came closer and put his one paw on my leg. Plan A was just to sit. Plan B was to put his paw on my leg. Now if that didn't work, plan C was to push down twice on my leg with his paw as if to say, "Hey, did you forget me?" Now if I still refused to give in, Maurice went to plan D. He would stand up on all four legs, jump backward, and bark at the same time as if to say, "Hey, you, what am I, chopped liver? Remember me? This is your loyal dog who keeps your lap warm on a cold winter night!"

If plans A through D didn't pull at my heartstrings and cause me to respond, Maurice persisted to the last plan. He would jump onto his favorite pillow but only after he positioned it just right to please him. He would close his eyes for a brief moment then quickly open them at the sound of my fork or spoon scraping the bottom of my plate.

Maurice would wait patiently but with great expectation. He prayed to receive even the crumbs from my meal. He lasted through the trial and persisted to the end, and his vision has finally been fulfilled. He receives the leftovers of my meal. How far are you willing to go? How many plans have you made to realize your visions in life? Many of us give up at plan A. Waiting with expectations for the final rewards is always the hardest plan. We live in a fast-moving society where waiting seems to be unacceptable and even negative.

I admire Joshua and Caleb in the Bible. They had a vision and believed it even when everyone around said it couldn't be done. These two young men didn't forget their vision of the land of milk and honey. For forty years, they traveled with people who told them it was impossible to obtain and possess the land. Joshua and Caleb persisted, and after forty years, their promise was fulfilled. In God's timing, all visions are possible.

Be still and know. Knowing is the easy part. But, be still? Many of us are like the child at the checkout counter with his mother. The child will yank and yank at mom to get the candy because he thinks he wants it. If mom is smart, she will make the child wait for something better like a fresh piece of fruit from the farmers' market. That would be much healthier for her son and worth his wait. God knows what is good for us better than we will ever know.

If we wait for God's timing, we can eat the fresh, unspoiled fruits that come from persistence and patience. I have been praying a long time for self-confidence, but only after many trials did I realize what God was already doing in my life without me ever knowing. Now I am finally seeing the rewards of my faithfulness and determination. .

For the first time in my life, at the age of forty-three, I had a definite vision and a purpose. Maybe it was triggered by a mid-life conversation I had with God. I asked the Lord, "What have I achieved in life so far?" and "Who have I helped in the process?" I have achieved a lot as far as raising a family, but I realized how much was still dormant waiting to be shared with others.

Learn these lessons now and get a vision for your life. There is no wrong age or time to receive a vision. My dog had just as much persistence and determination with only one good eye as when he was young and vibrant. Even when he blindly ran into doorways and furniture, he knew what he wanted, and he was willing to go to any length to get it.

My dog's favorite reward was licking the bottom of a bowl of ice cream. You are the cream in ice cream when you start believing and pursuing the vision God has given you. After all, cream rises to the top, doesn't it? Next time you eat ice cream, save the creamy bottom part for your dog, and remember you are the cream that rises.

I'd like to share an acronym for CREAM:

C   reate a vision and
R   each it by not
E   xisting until plans
A   through E are applied.
M   ay your dreams come true.

EVERYONE NEEDS TO KNOW A JIMMY

When I was fifteen years old, my mother started taking me to her adult prayer group. The people diligently prayed for me to be healed of epilepsy. Years later, at the age of twenty-nine, I received my healing from epilepsy.

The most fascinating person in that prayer group was Jimmy. Jimmy was a thirty-five-year-old man who was unable to walk without crutches. He was also very hard to understand with his slurred speech. Jimmy had cerebral palsy. He couldn't read, but miraculously he was able to read the Bible. Jimmy always had a smile and greeted me with love. The other members of the prayer group loved me too, but Jimmy was very special.

My epilepsy was pretty well under control by my last year of high school through mediation. I was allowed to walk in the March of Dimes walkathon. I had wanted to participate in this walkathon for years but couldn't without my doctor's permission. I was so excited to finally walk twenty miles and collect money for special people like Jimmy.

The big day came for the walk. Guess who I walked

with? That's right. Jimmy walked on crutches with me for five miles. He had to stop when his arms hurt him from the weight on his crutches. It began to rain. The rain was a blessing to us on that hot New York day for two reasons. The rain cooled us down and reduced the walk to only ten miles. Jimmy actually walked half way when he stopped after five miles.

Jimmy may not have been able to finish that walk, but to me he was and is a hero. His joy and determination even to attempt that walk overwhelmed me. It must have been very painful dragging both of his feet as he lifted himself with his crutches. Jimmy never shared any regrets from that walk. He only shared laughter and memories.

Shouldn't our lives be so fulfilled that even if there's a walk we can't finish on life's highway, we can be happy and share the experience in gladness? It's not the person that finishes first that is the only winner. The person that fails after he or she has attempted with determination is also a winner.

We are not all equal in our walks, so don't compare yourself to someone else and their abilities. Physically, there was a great difference between Jimmy and me, but mentally and spiritually, Jimmy won the award. Even Jesus had help carrying his cross to Calvary. What a victory Jesus had that nobody will ever forget.

Your crutches can either be problems in your life that stop you from trying, or they can be vehicles to motivate you. It's totally up to you. Crutches never stopped Jimmy from moving on. If you have never met a Jimmy in your life, seek out one to be your hero.

I left home at eighteen and lost contact with Jimmy. I did hear that Jimmy married, rides a three-wheel bike with his wife, and worked at the sheltered workshop in my hometown of Norwich, New York. Praise the Lord for the Jimmys of this world.

Seek deep inside yourself and find the determination to continue on. Don't walk alone. Someone needs your company, and you need their encouragement. The best thing we can give each other is a listening ear and words of encouragement.

I have walked other walkathons since that special one I walked with Jimmy. None of the other walks were ever as special as that one with my friend Jimmy. By the way, I did win the first prize for collecting the most money, but my best prize was Jimmy and his friendship.

An acronym for WALK:

W ith God
A ll trials are
L essons to be
K indled and shared.

USE ALL THE CRAYONS IN THE BOX

My favorite activity besides walking in the woods as a child was coloring or painting pictures of nature. I did best with flowers. I loved to use all different colors. As I grew up, I became more realistic and used only the colors I could see instead of using my imagination.

If you have ever watched children as they play with crayons, you have noticed that they use all the colors in the crayon box to make each creation of their imagination. Why? Children have no boundaries. Only adults set limitations. Children know how to dream and imagine the world in colors. Roses don't have to always be red. They can be pink polka dotted if you dream them to be.

It's because of dreams and childlike minds that we have inventions such as light bulbs, cars, and telephones. Are you a child at heart? Then be a child also in mind and spirit. The boundaries you set and your tunnel vision have to be removed in order to start using more crayons in the box.

My husband and I never dreamt we could own a home of our own. In November of 1984 our family moved from

New York State to Florida. The Lord impressed upon me to write in my yearly Christmas letter that we would have a home of our own in less than six months. We only were able to save $500 during our first six years of marriage. Believe it or not, we were able to buy a brand new home with that $500 as a down payment. We had to carry two mortgages. We moved into our new home in January of 1985.

Bill and I both had to work full time to keep our home. On the weekends and in our free time, we mowed lawns or cleaned condos. God never said he would give us a house. God said he would provide a way to get a house. Our dreams had come true, and God's promise had come to pass.

If you can dream it, you can do it. Of course there's a big *if* in that last statement. That dream can come true if that dream is in God's will for your life.

Don't have a Sarah spirit and try to go ahead of God. God promised Sarah that she would have a baby by her husband Abraham. Sarah became impatient with God when she didn't conceive a child as promised. Sarah then called on her maidservant to lay with Abraham to conceive a baby. Sarah did conceive a son but only after she tried to do God's job without him. If God says it will happen, it will. We have to learn to wait.

You may be saying, like Sarah said, "Wait? I'm too old to wait too long." May I remind you that Jesus lived thirty years before he turned the water into wine at the wedding at Canaan. That was his first miracle. His ministry of miracles was only seen for three years before he was crucified. Even if you are later in years, God can do great things in a short time. Imagine how you can impact this world before you to go and be with Jesus.

You are here on earth to glorify the Lord as you live, love, learn, and leave a legacy. Living means to spend all your waking hours enjoying your surroundings and God's people. Use every minute to praise the Lord.

Love is a verb. Love can be spoken, but it is best when performed. Love in its purest form is unconditional. Loving this way is hard because we are carnal beings.

Learn means trying all colors in the crayon box. It means you never stop asking questions or discovering new areas of life. The best learning device I have found in recent years is the Internet. I can learn anything and everything in the comfort of my home while sipping on a hot cup coffee.

Leave a legacy. We aren't all going to have our names written in our grandchildren's history books at school, but we can leave a legacy of love and compassion.

My grandparents moved to Norway from the United States during the Vietnam War era. I was only twelve years old at the time. They left me a legacy of love in the short time I spent with them. I especially remember my grandfather taking my cousin Lorry and me to the small country store in Mt. Upton, New York. Grandpa would buy both of us an ice cream cone or some candy. I thank God for those few years of memories.

Most of our grandchildren live outside the state of Florida. It has been very hard to establish a legacy with them. Financially we cannot afford many trips to visit them in Kansas, Pennsylvania, and New York. Most of our legacy is built during telephone calls.

My husband and I had the blessing and privilege to have a granddaughter and her mother live with us for three months. Madeline, who is now sixteen, gave us many wonderful memories in that short visit. Every time we talk with Madeline on the telephone, we ask her if she wants to come and see the bubbles in Florida. Madeline called the ocean waves bubbles when she was three years old.

You don't have to be famous to leave a legacy. You just have to make sure the legacy you leave is love. Dare to use all the crayons in the box and learn to dream. Don't just exist, live.

An acronym for CRAYONS is:

C   apture and
R   adiate the
A   wesome love of
Y   our Lord.
O   pen your mind and
N   ever stop learning.
S   eek to dream without limits.

ICE-SKATING LESSONS OF LIFE

I learned how to ice-skate when I was four years old. I practiced at the ice rink downtown and on the pond across the dirt road in front of our country home. I'm not a star, but I do pretty well, if I do say so myself. My mom named me after the Olympic ice skater Barbara Ann Scott. While learning to skate, I fell many times before I accomplished victory. I really don't remember the falls. I just remember being able to skate. Maybe I was too young to remember the falls, or maybe I chose to remember only the victory.

When I was in my late teens, I remember a bad fall I experienced. I was around seventeen years old when I learned how to roller-skate. I thought roller-skating would be easy since I already knew how to ice-skate. I didn't realize that I had to learn to skate a brand new way. When I learned to ice-skate, I skated straightforward instead of from side to side as most people do. This was due to the brief bout of polio I had on my right side as a child. The first try at roller-skating in the beginners' rink landed my body very quickly face down on the hard wooden floor. I fell more after that first awakening experience, but I knew then what I shouldn't do.

I became a fairly, good roller-skater. Every time I

would try a different move, such as going backward on skates or turning around, I would go through the process again of trying, discovering, falling, and getting up.

These lessons we have learned from our childhood are seldom used or applied to our life in the world of an adult. If you and I used the same determination to get up and try again in our adult lives as we did as a children, we would experience our rewards faster in life. Adults are too serious. I have become more childlike, thank God. It is so much easier to bounce back from my falls now.

When my daughter Sarah fell down as a child, she would look at me, then show me a big smile and jump right back up. She attempted over and over again to triumph over obstacles such as climbing a tree or beating her older sister in a race. Sarah never gave up. She tried again and again. My daughters' favorite song at the ages of four and six years old was "The Sun Will Come Out Tomorrow" from the musical *Annie*. My daughters taught me many lessons in persistence.

When life situations became larger for Sarah, she walked in confidence and a childlike faith in the Lord. Sarah was my baby. At the young age of sixteen, she became pregnant. She chose to keep her baby. Our grandson David is now ten years old. Sarah went from being an eleventh-grade cheerleader to being a mom and a wife all in one year. Sarah has kept her cheerleader attitude and childlike sweetness through every trial in her life.

Can you tell I'm a proud mother? By the way, Sarah is an excellent ice skater and roller-skater.

How about you? Can you bounce back after falling in the rink of life, or do you stay on the floor while others are trying to avoid running into you? Get up as fast as you can, and if you need help getting up, ask for it.

Next time you go skating, whether it is ice- or roller-skating, remember the lessons you are learning should be applied to your life as well. You may be in a different rink now, but the same rules apply: when you fall down, get up as soon as possible; try, try, and try again till you succeed.

An acronym for SKATE:

S   trive to
K   eep getting up
A   nd learn from
T   he many falls.
E   very day is an adventure.

IT'S TIME TO SEEK

When my husband and I watched *Mighty Joe Young*, I got a kick out of the scene where Mighty Joe Young played "Hide-N-Seek." This two-thousand-pound gorilla thought he could hide from his human friend Jill. Jill played along with Joe and pretended to not be able to find him right away. It was so cute.

I used to play "Hide-N-Seek" with my brothers on the farm. We had a large farmhouse with an attic, a second floor, and a basement with a pickle storage room. We also had a barn with two levels, a chicken coop, and many storage sheds. It took a long time to find my brothers, especially if we didn't make a limit as to what areas we could hide in.

My brothers and I also played a game called "Huckle Buckle Beanstalk" (also known as "hot or cold"). I have no idea where anyone came up with that name for a game, but the game was fun. Someone would hide a small object. Some of that object had to show partially. The person that hid the object would give clues of cold, warm, and hot. As the seekers got closer, the leader would call out "hotter."

Whenever we heard the word "cold," we turned completely in the opposite direction. When we heard "hot," all of us, no matter where we were in the room, would gather near the "hot" person. When someone saw the hidden object, they would shout out "Huckle buckle beanstalk" and win.

"Hide-N-Seek" involved no directions such as "hotter" or "colder." It did require good listening skills. Many times I could find someone after hearing a whisper or giggle. "Hide-N-Seek" took self-motivation and patience. I never would say "I give up." That would be like saying "I failed." No, I would continue looking for my brothers until they got tried of waiting.

With Huckle Buckle Beanstalk, I never had to worry about not finding the object. Directions were given of hotter and colder until the object was found. It usually took less than two minutes to find it. That was a game where it was easy to win if you could move fast and listen well.

Why am I telling you about these two childhood games? Because our lives are games of "Hide-N-Seek" and "Huckle Buckle Beanstalk." There are many hidden abilities in your lives. There are many talents that are hidden waiting to be found.

I have a beautiful daughter named Debbie who is blessed with many talents. As a teenager, she was an expressive, graceful dancer, a mime, and a spirit-filled singer. She is now an organized young lady, mother, and wife. Since she became a mother and a wife at eighteen years old, she has let some of those other talents hide. She knows where to find them. I pray some day she will.

How about you? How long will you stay cold? It's time to play the game. Listen closely to the directions, and you will be blessed and will bless others. It's your turn to seek. Like Joe, your talents are too big to hide. I'm sure Joe never considered himself as mighty. He simply loved playing the game. Enjoy the seeking. There are many Mighty Joe Youngs around each corner. Count to ten and go seek.

An acronym for GAMES:

G   o seek
A   nd find and
M   ake of your life
E   verything it
S   hould be.

WHAT MAKES A BARN A BARN?

The barn was one of my favorite havens to find peace during my childhood days. I especially loved going into the milk house and singing at the top of my lungs. The echo in there was beautiful, and it made me sound great. I was safe from insult there.

There was a smell to the barn that I was so used to that it never bothered me. What makes a barn a barn? It's not the cows on the first floor or the smell of hay and grain on the top floor. After all, if cows made a barn a barn, then do cows make a field a field? Well, let me tell you, manure is what makes a barn a barn.

As I was thinking about this picture of cow manure lining the gutters in the barn, I received an analogy from God. The barn is representative of our bodies, and the manure represents the many, many trials we have to go through in our lifetime.

Do you know what we used to do with the manure from our barn? We would shovel it into a manure spreader and spread it in the fields as fertilizer. It made the fields and the crops grow bigger and better. I also remember using the manure as fertilizer for our garden. I don't live on a farm now, but I can buy dried manure in almost any garden center. We don't pay money for our trials, but we can use our trials as fertilizer for our lives. Don't let the trials stay in your barn. They will overflow the gutters and stink out the whole barn. You need to daily take the manure spreader and shovel out the trials. Use your trials to grow a stronger you. The barn will always have gutters because there will always be manure. You must keep your barn clean to keep it operational.

May of 1998 when I traveled up to New York State to be with my dying father, I saw a disturbing sight at our old farmhouse. I had lived at that farmhouse and played in that barn for the first seventeen years of my life. Just one week before I arrived in New York State, there had been a fire at the old barn. It burned to the ground. There were only two things remaining. The cement foundation and the cement gutters. The gutters were empty and odorless. It was no longer a barn.

I believe we leave the gutters of trials behind when we go to be with our Maker. As the barn had an end to its usefulness, so we too will come to a time in our lives here on earth. Our structure will become weak and return to dust. We will no longer have need for earthly things. When we go to our Maker, our trials will dissolve and become odorless just like the manure in the old burned down barn in New York State.

Next time you walk into a barn of any kind, let those smells remind you of the trials in your life that were and will be good fertilizer and preparation for your soul.

An acronym for MANURE:

M   any and frequent
A   re the unexpected,
N   everending, but
U   seful trials that
R   aise you to
E   ven higher levels.

SMILEY HAPPY FACES

One of the things I vividly remember from my teen years was smiley faces. You know? The bright yellow round faces with black eyes and a big black smile. Smiley faces were on everything from t-shirts to key chains to bed sheets. You name it. It had a smiley face on it.

It had been almost a year since my dad went to the golden ice-skating rinks of heaven. My dad is now whole and able to skate again and enjoy his new life. When he died the May of 1998, the Lord led me to give my mother, brothers, sister-in-law, and nieces little smiley face angel pins. I kept one too. I feel a heart connection with my precious relatives because of that pin.

There's a special song from *The Sound of Music* that should have smiley faces added to its lyrics. That song is called "My Favorite Things." It goes: "Raindrops on roses and whiskers on kittens, bright copper kettles and warm woolen mittens. Brown paper packages tied up with string. These are a few of my favorite things." The song tells you to think about your favorite things when bad things happen in your life.

This song became quite a bond between my then nine-year-old niece, Alysia, and I in May of 1998 when my dad died. Her father, my brother, was having a hard time with her grandpa's death. Alysia and her little sister, Andi, ran upstairs. I followed them, took their hands, and then we kneeled and prayed. I then taught them that song. Before I returned to Florida from New York, I taught Alysia every word, and she taught her class at school. Alysia emails me once in a while just to say, "I love you." That smiley face angel pin reminds me of how God uses bad events in our lives to work for his good. My father's death brought us closer.

Something happened in April of 1999 that prompted me once again to buy a smiley face object. My then nineteen-year-old daughter, Debbie, had a miscarriage in her third month of pregnancy. She lived in North Carolina, and I lived in Florida. I wanted so badly to be able to hug her. I wanted to lay her down on my lap like I used to and comb her beautiful, long blonde hair as I scratched her back. Since I couldn't be there, the Lord led me to write her an encouraging letter and buy her a smiley face stuffed toy.

The computer program I use at home has smiley faces ☺ built in. Of course these smiley faces aren't in color, but I love to type them anyway. I also love to sign all birthday and get well cards with a smiley sun face. It has become my trademark.

I have some missionary friends in Jamaica. Tommy and Sandi always have smiles painted on their faces. In April of 1999, Tommy emailed us here in the United States and asked for prayer for himself and the people of Jamaica. That week three men were hung in the gallows for their crimes. Take a trip to Jamaica, and you will wear a smiley face every day when you realize how many blessings you have here as an American. As Tommy would say, "Hey, mon. Don't worry, be happy. God is in control. It only gets gooder and gooder."

If you don't have a bright, yellow, smiley face of any kind, look in the mirror and smile from cheek to cheek. It will encourage you and others around you. I promise. Smile, God loves you, and so do I.

An acronym for SMILE:

S   et your eyes on Jesus and
M   ake him Lord
I   n your life.
L   ook in the mirror and
E   mit a smile.

IS BIGGER REALLY BETTER

In the fall of 1999, the population in our house increased to seven. My stepdaughter, Mary Beth, and her family moved down from New York State. Mary Beth had another child due that November. Our grandchildren Madeline, seven years old; Micah, five years old; and Katelynn, two years old, were bundles of energy. They were with us for a season.

All seven of us went grocery shopping one day. Besides the essentials, we also bought a $1.99 watermelon. We couldn't wait to get it home and eat it. By the time we arrived home, the children were ready for bed. We decided to wait and eat the watermelon the next day.

The next afternoon at lunchtime, my son-in-law Mike offered me some watermelon. We both commented on how good it was. Both of us agreed that the bigger melons weren't as juicy or as tasty as the smaller ones. Is bigger always better? I thought about this question as I ate my watermelon.

We work hard all of our lives to get bigger homes and more toys. I remember a free five-day cruise our family received. We went with other Christian friends to Mexico, and handed out little Spanish Bibles to the

Mexicans in the back streets of Cozumel, Mexico. Our children gave their own stuffed toy animals to the children who lived there. The Mexican people were overjoyed and thanked us in Spanish as we walked the narrow streets.

Most of their homes were tiny huts with dirt floors. They were so happy and smiley. How could this be? I guess "a house does not a home make" was true for them. This really came alive to our family on that cruise.

One hot summer day, I became very thirsty during my lunch hour. I decided to buy a bean burrito and a large soda. I should have bought a small soda because I knew I couldn't finish a large one. The bigger-size soda was on sale. It would have been dumb to get the smaller soda right? Wrong.

I discovered after I bought the soda that my car's cup holder wasn't big enough to hold the bigger drink. I decided to hold it with one hand. As I drove with the other hand, I encountered a problem. When turning the corner and trying to navigate my car, I almost lost control. I needed two hands to control the car wheel, so I let go of my drink to avoid an accident. Bigger wasn't better. I spent the rest of my lunch hour soaking up sticky soda from the rug of my car.

As our incomes increase, so do our toys, don't they? Our toys are such things as a new pool, a boat, and motorcycles. You get the idea. Is bigger really better? God says if we are faithful with a little, he will give us more. Usually he allows the increase so we can help others rather than ourselves.

We desire to have enough money to help others in bigger ways someday. We are on the receiving side of the giving cycle right now. I believe in time God will honor our desire. Bigger can be better, but only when the increase comes from God and when it isn't for selfish desires. Next time you pick out a watermelon at the store or dream about bigger things, remember bigger isn't always better.

An acronym for BIGGER:

B   est to desire to
I   nvest in your family and
G   ive than to be
G   reedy and
E   arn nothing but
R   ust on your toys.

STAY FOCUSED

I n 1999 when I started my spring-cleaning, I began with my freezer. I disposed of a few items from my freezer that had definitely extended their stay. I took yet another item from the freezer and defrosted it. It was a twenty-five-pound turkey.

We helped our daughters and their families move to Fort Pierce, Florida, the week of Fourth of July. On the Fourth of July weekend, we decided to cook the defrosted bird. I cooked it five hours at our home then transported the turkey, two homemade apple pies, and homemade banana bread to Fort Pierce for a Fourth of July celebration. That turkey was so tender that it fell apart when I lifted it from the pan to make gravy.

Let me take you back to a year earlier in May of 1998. In one week, I experienced more mental stress than I had felt my entire life. During that week in May 1998, my husband and I were threatened by a loved one with bodily harm, my husband and I transported my dying father to New York State for final goodbyes, we found out my sixteen-year-old daughter was six months pregnant, that same daughter moved out of the house to her sister's, and I watched my dad in a coma for five days. The hospital in New York State allowed my brothers and me to remove my dad's life support. I know God never gives us more than we can handle, but I thought God must have overestimated my breaking point that time.

One of the best lessons I learned during this week is still useful in my daily thinking. My oldest brother, Russell, kindly told me to drop any worry about my pregnant daughter and stay focused on the issue at hand. I was very offended and thought my brother had too little concern about my family and its crisis. I could do nothing for Sarah who was miles away in New Smyrna Beach, Florida. I was in New York State. Russell's advice was correct and did benefit me in dealing more rationally with my father's death.

When I returned to Florida I changed my focus once again. This time my focus was on Sarah and her child to be. That doesn't mean I forgot about my family in New York State and Texas still healing from my dad's death. I emailed my brothers almost every day to encourage them and to receive encouragement. I also published my dad's tribute in the local newspaper. I hope I have conveyed to each one of you that focus doesn't literally mean concern. The best way to know what to focus on is to pray. I automatically tell myself to stay focused throughout the workday. My stress level has decreased greatly using this daily practice. Try it sometime.

After the wonderful turkey dinner and time of bonding with my daughters and their families on the Fourth of July in Fort Pierce, Florida, I rode back home with my daughter Sarah's in-laws. While we were loading the van, Sarah's husband received some last words of wisdom from his father. Then his mother (well, actually stepmother but very close and special to him) gave him an added pearl of wisdom. That short and simple pearl was "stay focused."

Remember the lesson about focus the next time you spring clean. Cook up that piece of meat in the freezer and share it with someone you love. Create a memory, and most of all stay focused.

An acronym for FOCUS:

F   ind your priorities and
O   nly seek to
C   oncentrate on them.
U   nique is each
S   ituation, so pray.

WATCH OUT FOR THE FIB

my television habits changed greatly in 1999 when my grandchildren and their parents came to live with us for a while. At 8:00 p.m., I was invited by Madeline, Micah, and Katelynn to join them on the sofa for a video of VeggieTales. VeggieTales, for those of you without children or grandchildren, are videos of vegetable characters that teach good moral issues in a fun way. Katelynn the two-year-old could sit still for almost an hour watching these videos.

One night we all watched a VeggieTale about Fib, a little purple vegetable who coaxed another veggie into telling a lie. That little lie then grew bigger and bigger as the veggie fibbed more and more to cover up his first lie. Before the veggie knew it, the cute little purple Fib was bigger than the water tower. The Fib almost killed the veggie who created him. Then the veggie told the truth, and the Fib slowly shrunk until it finally disappeared. Do we ever invite that little purple Fib monster into our lives? It only takes one small fib to start him growing.

We are programmed as young children that a fib will keep us out of trouble—for a short time at least. For example: A child is asked by his parent to brush his teeth. The parent then asks the child if he brushed his teeth. That child says "yes" but really didn't brush his teeth.

That's a lie. Then even if the child wanted to brush his teeth later he can't. He would be caught in the fib.

Now let's look at parents. The phone rings. You just sat down on the sofa, put your legs up, and started sipping on a large glass of iced tea. You ask your child to get the phone for you. You discover the person on the other end is someone you really don't want to talk to right now. You say to your child, "Tell him I'm not available." A fib has started to grow. You are also teaching your children right from wrong.

Sometimes the truth doesn't feel good, but anything has to be better than being eaten up by a fib. Every time I finish writing a story in rough draft, I read it to my husband and ask for his corrections and comments. At first he was very hesitant about telling me the whole truth. He remembered the days when I couldn't and wouldn't take correction of any kind. Praise the Lord, I have changed. Now my husband lovingly tells me the whole truth and nothing but the truth.

Being willing to accept the truth sometimes hurts. It's kind of like going to doctor for a shot. You know it will hurt, but you also know it is good medicine. After the initial pain, you can rest and let your body do the healing.

Teach your children by your example. All the VeggieTale videos ever made will mean nothing to your child unless you lead by your example. Practice what you preach.

An acronym for TRUTH:

T   ell your children to
R   esist the "Fib."
U   nder no circumstances
T   ell a lie, but
H   old tight to the truth.

DO YOU REALLY KNOW SOMEONE

Turks is a show about a close-knit family. Everyone in the family is a cop except for the mother. In one episode, one of the sons befriended an old man after the old man experienced a home invasion. The old man composed beautiful cello music and played like a professional. The young cop couldn't understand why the old man wasn't angry with the invader.

The old man posed two questions to the young cop. The cop answered without really thinking. The questions were, "How do you know if a person is good or bad?" and, "Can you look at some children playing at a playground and tell which ones are bad?"

The young cop said without hesitation, "Yes, I can." As the show continued, the young cop discovered something about his new friend that stunned him. The precious, talented old man had served time for murdering his wife in a fit of anger years ago.

The old man, aware that the cop knew about him, asked the young cop, "Does knowing this information about me change the caring friendship we have developed?" Before the old man died of a heart attack, he urged the young cop to forgive his own father and love him unconditionally. This young cop's own father had had an affair with a younger woman. Until the young cop met this old man, forgiveness was not possible.

All have sinned and fallen short of the glory of God. I made a decision that ended someone's life too. I gave up my precious gift of purity and became pregnant when I was nineteen years old. It was my first time, but that's all it took. A close family member urged me to have an abortion. The state of New York even paid for it through the state welfare system. It was the worst decision I ever made.

There is not a year that goes by that I don't think of my son being a year older. I shared my testimony with my daughters when they were young, and I shared with the church youth group. I thank God I had the courage to risk rejection in sharing my testimony. One of the young girls in youth group became pregnant at the age of fifteen. She shared with me how my testimony saved her little girl from an abortion. This girl's boyfriend had the money and offered to pay for an abortion.

When my own two daughters were sixteen and eighteen years old, they became pregnant. I'd like to think that my testimony also helped them make the right decision. I was blessed with two beautiful grandsons that year. Your shared testimony is important.

It took me ten long years to forgive myself of that abortion. I knew God had forgiven me. To forgive myself was harder. At age twenty-nine, I named my baby in heaven Daniel and laid him to rest. There was something about giving my baby a name that brought closure and self-forgiveness.

Like the old man on the television show, I too had

things in my past that for years I feared someone would find out about. I am truly grateful that God has given me the strength and courage to now share this tragedy with others in order to prevent even more tragedies.

If you are truthful, you too could give a testimony of lessons you have learned from some tragic and wrong decisions you made in the past. God will give you the strength. Make sure you testify of these lessons learned.

Somebody needed me to write this story and share my life. Someone needs to hear your testimony too. Even if only one person is affected by hearing your testimony, it is well worth the risk. God sent the Good Shepherd after just one sheep when that sheep was lost. That one is important.

Think of how many of you mothers and fathers would be grandparents if your child had heard a testimony from someone who knew the pain and the truth. Parents aren't perfect. They never will be perfect. Share with your children about the mistakes you made in the past. Also share with your children the mistakes you still make. Then accept the mistakes they make and love them as God loves you, unconditionally.

An acronym for TESTIFY:

T   ell of your
E   rrors and
S   hare your
T   imes of defeat.
I   n all situations
F   ocus on God's goodness.
Y   ou aren't perfect.

FORTS OF LOVE

One Sunday morning at church, I was watching two of our church members climb up and down the ladders to hang linen drapes to give us privacy from the outside. There were many windows in the school cafeteria. It was almost like building a giant fort.

I remember building smaller forts with my girlfriends when I was a child. We would take bed sheets and blankets and drape them over chairs, beds, and tables to make a private fort. It usually took us half the day to construct our fort. We had fun in the fort for a couple of hours before my mom called us to come and eat dinner, take a bath, and go to bed. Before dinner we had to take down the fort and clean up. All that hard work just to have Mom say, "It's time to clean up your bedroom."

That fort was a special place where my friends and I told secrets and discussed important girl things. We had an original name for our club. It was called "The Girls' Club." There were only three members, including myself, in our club. We always had a good time.

My family lived in the country, so there weren't many little girls my age in my neighborhood to play with. The houses were far apart. The two girls that belonged to our club lived about a forth of a mile down our dirt road. We graduated from our forts to a little, old storage shed in the flower garden when we were older. Somehow the old shed just didn't feel as secure as the forts even though it was much more permanent and sturdy.

When we had to take down the forts in our house, each time we felt a closure to our special moments. We also felt a security that our secrets were safely folded away with the sheets and blankets. In the old shed, I almost felt like the walls absorbed our secrets, and who knows, maybe walls do talk. The shed was so solid and immovable.

Our church was like my girls' club fort. At my church on Wednesday nights and Sunday mornings, each member had a part in constructing our fort. Our church fort only stayed up a couple of hours. Each church member, like each member of our girls' club, took pride in their part of the creation.

Our church has items of both the shed and the fort. It's in a concrete building, but with some creativity, it can be made into a place of comfort and a time to share secrets with your heavenly Father. When the drapes come down at the end of the service, all our burdens and cares have been taken care of.

Our hearts are like forts and churches. A heart has chambers that can be full of many burdens and secrets. Your heart is where Jesus lives. If you have a hard heart, you become very concrete and immovable. Your heart can even break with enough pressure. On the other hand, if you have a heart like a linen fort you will be flexible and useable. You will be able to withstand many winds and storms.

Someday soon take time to build a fort with your

kids, grandkids, or even just with you and your spouse. It may sound silly, but don't laugh until you have tried it. In fact, take some ice cream bars (fudge bars are the best) or hot drinks (kids love hot chocolate) into the fort with you, then relax and be open with each other.

When our family had tent meetings in forts, we were amazed at the unforgettable things we might talk about. There is something special and comfortable about a fort.

An acronym for HEART:

H ard hearts
E lect to
A ct negatively.
R est in a fort and
T urn your heart soft.

HOW MANY ACRES HAVE YOU EXPLORED

I liked sitting in my bedroom for moments of solitude. As I sat on the floor and leaned up against my bed, I would see a special stick of wood. I saved this stick after my dad died. It was a keepsake to remind me of the valuc of exploration. My dad used the bare wooden stick that is about the thickness of a silver dollar to help him walk in the woods. He never walked anywhere without it. In fact he kept it and other important articles such as fifty-year-old ice skates in his car trunk at all times just in case the need arose.

Until I started writing these stories, I didn't realize how much like my dad I really was. I have always loved nature. I loved nature just as much if not more than my dad did. Between the ages of seven and seventeen, I took many walks in nature. My family owned 350 acres of meadows, farmland, and woods. I liked to go across the pasture that was located about one-forth of a mile from our farmhouse. I would cross the pasture and enter the woods with its tall majestic trees. I would fearlessly climb the hill and crush fallen dried leaves and broken branches as I approached the slate rock cliffs.

I knew the direction I had to climb to reach the large hay fields at the top of the hill. I had no idea what obstacles of nature might await me on my walk. With childlike faith and enthusiasm, I continued up the hill with a spirit of expectancy. I knew that if I was very quiet and careful, I could peek through the foliage of the woods at the top of the hill and see a family of deer. They would be standing in the sunlit field grazing on hay.

The walk was long across the open hay fields. It seemed to be the longest part of my journey. One reason might be because I could see where I was going. There was no mystery of the next step and what it might bring.

The field ended and the woods began again as I headed downward toward the farmhouse. I would have a choice to make. I could go down the same way I had always gone, or I could explore yet another trail in the woods. I usually took the new trail and discovered yet more wonders of nature.

My last stop was always at the small pond at the bottom of the tractor trail. The pond sometimes became a home to wild ducks. I would pick some wild flowers or cattails to bring to my mom. Sometimes I would surprise Mom with some pollywogs and salamanders. Why did I take you for this journey? The journeys or walks I took as a child are still continuing today only not at the farm. Of the 350 acres of land that God had allowed me to travel as a child, I think I must have traveled at least 300.

God has now placed you and me in a bigger arena of life. This arena is much bigger than those acres of land in New York State. How much of your new adventure land have you explored? I have just started my new adventures, and I have found them as rewarding as the fearless walks I used to take during my childhood.

Adventure and discovery never stop unless you choose to stay at home and lock the doors. Fear can make you a victim. It can steal your creativity and smother your dreams.

Get on your hiking boots and explore the woods and hayfields of life. Explore the hills and the valleys of life. Dr. Martin Luther King Jr. said it well in 1963 on the steps of the Lincoln Memorial: "I have a dream." You too must not only have a dream, but also as Dr. King did, strive to make that dream a reality.

An acronym for DREAM:

D   on't be robbed of the
R   ichness of your dreams.
E   ver seek to bring
A   live your dream and
M   ake it reality.

EGOR THE DUCK

While my husband and I were taking a quiet, peaceful walk together on the beach one day, we spotted two egrets. One was standing on the sand, and the other was standing in a beach lounge chair. Both were standing tall and acting as if that was their territory. The real occupants of that lounge chair and space were out swimming and boogie boarding in the waves of the ocean. They were oblivious to the egret's residency there. The egret standing on the lounge chair turned and looked at me crossly, as if to say, "What are you looking at?"

On the car ride home from the beach that day, my childhood memories took me back to our manmade lake and some of its inhabitants. Our family had four beautiful white ducks as pets that made their home in our twenty-two acre lake. The duck I remember the most we called Egor. He was very friendly as he waddled right up to us and ate from our hands. Egor was special. We had a relationship and an understanding that if I took care of him and loved him, he wouldn't fly away. I don't remember if he flew away or died, but Egor did eventually leave.

Our family moved to Florida five years after Bill and

to daycare at the church each day while I worked a forty-
cial times, Sarah and I met some special friends. Sarah is

We made friends with three pelicans. We named
Egor. I had to get Egor in there somehow. We named
head I say hello to Pete, Pauline, and Charlie. I still see
Egor and his friends off the north bridge too.

All this talk about ducks and gooney birds is to say
inside and make you smile even if nobody is near at the
at the beach caused me to feel warm inside. It triggered
Sarah will share these memories with her children and

This walk on the beach also encouraged me to make

"Who would you like to surprise?" My daughter Debbie's response was "Daddy, when he gets better." Daddy had fallen and broken his neck. We had to cancel his surprise birthday party in November of 1991.

If your children are grown, then encourage them to save for your grandchildren's scrapbook of memories. If your children don't have children, sit down sometime with your children over coffee or tea and share a living scrapbook with them. Memories are important, so make sure you pass on these warm fuzzies.

An acronym for MEMORIES is:

M   ake use of
E   very moment to create
M   emories that will
O   pen up minds and
R   adiate a warm
I   nner peace.
E   very day is a
S   pecial memory in some way.

WHAT DOES THAT HAVE TO DO WITH LIFE

How do you feel about algebra? I realize many of you don't like and have never liked math, algebra, or any related subjects. What if I restate that question to say, "How do you feel about challenges?" My college algebra teacher received the same negative reactions while surfing in Costa Rica on spring break. She told some new friends that she was a math teacher. They stopped short and changed the subject. What is it about math that intimidates and scares us?

My first semester back in college was extremely challenging. I registered for both college algebra and macroeconomics. I needed to take both of these courses to work toward my degree. I had procrastinated at registering for classes and those courses were the only two available at the time. I learned a cute poem about procrastination years ago from a friend. It goes like this: "Procrastinate, procrastinate. Delay it until a later date. Put off the things you hate. Wait, wait, wait."

After signing up for my courses, I decided I would make the most out of a dreaded subject. I started my course in algebra expecting to do my best. After my first test in algebra, I felt like quitting, but I'm not a quitter. I hate failure I spent hours reviewing. I also started going to the learning center of the college. I would spend every free moment I could with a tutor. It had been twenty-five years since I had taken any kind of math course. I knew I would have to work harder than most of the young adults who had just finished taking the previous algebra class.

Many times during the duration of this class, I would ask myself, "What does algebra have to do with life?" Why is every student, no matter what field they are going into, required to take college algebra? My answer to these questions did come.

Have you ever had to do something you hated to do, but you did it anyway? If you said no, you're a liar. It may not be a college math course. It may be something as simple as ironing the clothes. It may be a more complex decision like deciding whether to move your ill parent into your home for a period of time.

Some of the things we dislike aren't really choices at all. They are responsibilities. Others are choices. It's much easier to procrastinate and delay a decision to a later date. Unfortunately the challenge won't go away. If you don't iron for a month, you will run out of clothes to wear or have to wear wrinkled clothes.

When I chose to go back to college, I was aware I would have to concentrate hard to achieve the desired goals I had set for myself. This required a giant step of confidence. I had to believe in my abilities as a middle-aged student and full-time employee that I could succeed. After starting my winter semester in January of 2000, both of my daughters and their husbands and children came to live with us for a brief period of time. Study was a challenge with a full house.

My grandson Ryan wanted to climb on top of my lap and study with me. I let him study algebra with me when I studied at home. When I wasn't at the college receiving tutoring or at home studying, I would study in my car at the river or ocean or under the large oak tree in the park.

We all make decisions and set goals every day. We decide what to eat, when to eat, what to wear, when to get up, what to react to, how much time to give to different people during the day, and so on. You get the idea. Each decision does change your day in the long run. In the short run each task may seem feeble.

I was glad I had taken that math course. I completed college algebra with an A. I not only thank God for completion of my course, but I also praise God for the lessons learned. Algebra taught me determination. I also redeveloped my study habits, and it taught me that even middle-aged people can use help from younger tutors.

One of my tutors at the college learning center was a classmate of my daughter. She had the knowledge of algebra that I needed. Algebra also taught me humility. One more thing it taught me was the ability to reason out problems and apply a formula to come to a solution.

God has given us a tutor to life's challenges. It is the Bible. Within its pages are all the answers you will ever need to apply to the daily challenges of life. Just reading my algebra book would not help me pass that class. Without ever applying the teaching to solve the problems, I would have failed.

My algebra teacher had another story she shared with us about her young son's t-ball team. She was coaching first base. She had the responsibility to tell the boys to go or stop at first base. She did her part, but the boys in their excitement ran right past her when she shouted stop. Are we any different from those young boys when it comes to getting carried away with emotion rather than applying knowledge and listening skills?

On the instruction sheet my algebra teacher handed out at the beginning of our course, number eleven was "no whining or complaining." Let's put that on our instruction list for all our challenges. I did complain once or twice. Ms. Saylor was so patient with all of us. That class was a challenge for her too. One of the last things Mrs. Saylor asked me just before the final exam was: "What makes some students study and others not even care?" I told her that I believe it lies in the goals each one of us set for ourselves. I tend to set mine high. How about you? How are you at studying? When is the last time you picked up your Bible and not only read it but studied and applied its teachings?

You see now what algebra has to do with life and life's challenges don't you? And you thought this was going to be a boring story. See you at finals.

An acronym for "ALGEBRA":

A ll trials are
L earning experiences and
G ive you the
E nergy to continue and
B ecome more trained to
R espond in the
A ccurate way more often.

YOU CAN RIDE OVER GOLIATH

One Friday night, my husband and I went to a monthly potluck supper with a group of special friends. We experienced a Via De Cristo (Way of Christ) weekend together and kept in touch with monthly gatherings. We sat with some friends we hadn't seen in almost two years. They had moved to North Carolina. This weekend they came back to New Smyrna Beach, Florida, to visit. The wife made a comment about how she longed to be back in New Smyrna Beach. She went into detail about the wonderful sensation she and her husband feel every time they come over the south bridge and head for their beachside condo. She said when they reach the top of the bridge they look upon the beautiful terrain below and the ocean in the distance as they travel down the bridge to reach what they still call home on South Atlantic Avenue.

Our family moved from New York State to Florida in 1984 on a wing and a prayer. When my daughters reached the ages of ten and twelve, we would take long bikes rides together. We enjoyed looking at the beauty of Florida as we pedaled our bikes. One of my favorite paths was traveling from Florida Shores to Riverside Drive about four miles away. Then we would ride slow

Barbara Mudge

and steady to the south bridge in New Smyrna Beach another five miles away. When we reached the bridge our real challenge began.

I promised the girls a Slurpee (a sweet, frozen ice drink) from 7-Eleven after we traveled up and over the south bridge. Half way up the bridge, we would lose our strength to pedal. We got off our bikes and, for a short distance, walked our bikes to the top. At the top we enjoyed the view before coasting down the bridge. We knew that if we could make it to the top of the bridge, we could reach our goal of Slurpees. Coasting down was the easy part of the journey.

Our first long bike trip was the hardest. My daughters complained a lot about the difficulty of the path we had chosen. I told them to think of this huge bridge as Goliath and to think of ourselves as little Davids. "You can defeat Goliath," I told them. "He just looks big and scary, but we can do it. Let's go."

We got our Slurpees, and then we headed back to home. The ride back seemed easier even though it was the same path. One thing my girls discovered was that this wasn't the only Goliath they would ever have to ride over.

Do you set your mind to defeat Goliath every day? Goliath represents any and all trials in your life that seem too difficult to conquer. We are made more than conquerors. We've been made victorious through the blood of Jesus Christ.

Next time you ride over a bridge, look out upon the vision of victory, and remember you can and will defeat Goliath. You will enjoy your coast to victory. Our friends desire to move back to New Smyrna Beach, but part of

138

their Goliath right now is the path of endurance that God has set for them in North Carolina.

Our rides were short compared to some of the trials we have faced. The longest bike ride my daughters and I endured was four hours long. That seems short compared to months and even years of endurance and prayer to defeat some of our Goliaths. All things do work for good. God said he would make all things beautiful in his time.

I have been very proud of my daughters for the Goliaths they have already challenged and defeated in their lives. My daughters at the age of sixteen and eighteen were challenged daily. They were young, teenage mothers and wives.

I believe the lessons learned on the bike rides gave them courage to be victorious no matter what Goliath came into their paths. I challenge each one of you to meet your Goliaths, such as financial problems, family problems, goals set but never acted upon, fear of people, fear of rejection, and fear of failure. There are a lot of Goliaths out there, aren't there? But you are a conqueror in Christ Jesus, so go forth and conquer.

An acronym for CONQUEROR is:

C   hallenge Goliath.
O   mit the fear and stay
N   estled in God's will.
Q   uitting is not allowed.
U   nite with God's strength and
E   ver be victorious.
R   est in your victory glide, and
O   n the journey always
R   ejoice and praise the Lord.

YOU'RE SMARTER THAN THAT

On July 1, 2000, as I was leaving the church, my pastor shook my hand and wished me a happy Fourth of July. My response was "Thank you, but I don't really have time to enjoy my day off. I'll be studying most of the day for my final in statistics." Then he surprised me with his reply of "You're smarter than that." For only a few seconds I thought, *What did he mean by that? Is he calling me stupid?*

That summer I had been taking a statistics class at Daytona Beach Community College. I had a low B average at that time. Only the final test remained. This test was the only thing that could bring my grade up to an A. I felt I needed to use all my free time to succeed in my goal. Yes, I am somewhat of a perfectionist.

All I could think of when my pastor said, "Have a good Fourth of July," was that I would have a whole day off work to start studying for my final. I was shocked by my pastor's statement so much that I realized what I had been thinking was completely wrong.

Sometimes I feel like Silly Putty, that clay ball that came in a colored, plastic egg container? I would take it into my hands and squeeze it. Then I would stretch it to make it big enough to copy a printed picture from the newspaper. The Sunday comic strips were the best to copy because they copied in color.

I liked stretching the putty with the copied picture to see how distorted and unrecognizable the picture became. Then I would squeeze the putty in my hands again and repeat the process over and over again. I was seeking that perfect picture.

I can become like that Silly Putty when I desire so much to achieve a grade of A that my vision becomes distorted. I momentarily forget that my family is the number one priority in my life. Nothing should ever take higher priority.

I have seen firsthand how video games can become obsessive and can distort the importance of family. I watched this father become angry with his two-year-old son for interrupting his video game. He was giving his son second place without even knowing he was doing it. This should not be.

Priorities for every one of us should be God first and family second. Church should be third, and everything else (studying, video games) should be last on our priority list. Studying for my statistics final should have been at the bottom of my priority list. Are your priorities in order?

Silly Putty is fun, but don't let your desire for perfection distort your true priorities in life. Life is much too short to worry about the least of our priorities. Become a Silly Putty reflection of peace, love, joy, patience, gentleness, and self-control.

Our family enjoyed a wonderful day of fun on the Fourth of July that year. We started our fun events with a swim at our daughter's swimming pool at her new apartment complex. Then we enjoyed cooking spiedies (only people from Binghamton, New York, will know what these are) on the grill. Spiedies are made by cutting pork tenderloin into cubes and marinating those cubes in a special "New York State Fair Spiedie Sauce," which could be bought in Binghamton, New York, area. After our picnic, we all went to the park by the river and sat on the crushed shells to watch the fireworks. The only thing distracting us from time-to-time was the approaching army of tiny sand crabs. It was a day to remember.

An acronym for STUPID is:

S   etting family
T   o the back and
U   nderstanding not the
P   riorities of life.
I   nsisting on
D   oing it your way.

WAIT FOR ME

When my daughters Debbie and Sarah were only two and four years old, they had a favorite 45 record they begged me to play for them. This single song recording was "Ten Little Indian Boys." My daughters loved to count with the song, but their favorite part was when the last little Indian boy, who was lagging behind, cried out, "Wait for me." My daughters would echo in their high voices. We would play that record over and over again. They had no idea that I was teaching them how to count. Tricky, aren't I?

When I was a young girl, I spent a lot of my time alone. There were a couple of times, however, I remember asking my father and brothers if I could be a part of their sports activities. I received injuries both times.

The first time I was allowed to play with my brothers was on a cool Sunday afternoon in New York State. I persisted in asking my brothers and father to let me play tackle football with them. After nagging and nagging, I was placed in the front line of the game right across from my oldest brother Russell. He was a good size larger than I, and he wore his eyeglasses even when he played sports. During one of the very first plays of the game, Russ and I met face to face after the ball was hiked to the quarterback. His eyeglasses gashed me right under my beautiful blue eye. I was taken out of the game and received stitches at the emergency room.

I also insisted on playing softball with my brothers. They had no problem letting me play in the outfield. They just didn't want me to be the pitcher. Being the determined young girl I was, I continued to insist on being pitcher. Finally after half the game was over, my brother Russ convinced the others to let me try the position of pitcher. My brother Russ was at bat as I threw an almost perfect ball. Russ connected so well that the ball came straight back at me on the pitcher mound. The ball hit me in my mouth. I received six stitches inside my mouth.

Many times in life when we feel like we are being left behind or unwanted, it simply is our lack of self-esteem or pride that causes us to insist on participating. I remember the time my desire to be included caused me to be falsely accused. I was eighteen and in college. I liked spending my free time at the student recreation center playing ping pong and card games. One day some buddies decided to have a party. I didn't have a driver's license, so I grabbed a ride from someone and joined the party.

Half way into the party, the others decided to smoke some weed and pass some barbiturates. I refused both but remained at the party because I didn't want to walk home in the dark alone. My comment to my buddies was "I have to take 750 milligrams of barbiturates a day to control my epileptic seizures. I don't need or want your five-milligram pills or your weed."

I lived at the YWCA at that time. When I finally arrived home from the party just before curfew, I was accused of smoking weed simply because my clothes reeked of it. I only went to one of those parties, by the way. I wasn't missing anything.

A second incident happened during my college days. I was working in the duplicating center through the work-study program. I loved the job, but I still had a need to be with the gang. Across from the duplicating center was a photography room where a fun-loving, middle-aged man named John developed photos for the college. One day he and five other workers in that building decided to go out for pizza at lunch. I was surprised and excited when they invited me.

I was so excited that I didn't think twice when I closed the door to the duplicating center and ran around the corner to catch a ride with them to the pizza parlor. When I returned after less than an hour, I found one angry employer. I had left the door unlocked to the room with nobody inside. I guess I must have forgotten that my boss and her assistant were at lunch when I mind-lessly decided to be a part of the gang. I lost a job I loved that day. The pizza and the gang really weren't worth the loss, but I did learn a good lesson.

I have become more able to accept a given position in the field now, and I don't insist on my way as much. The little Indian boy that yelled "wait for me" on the record never did catch up with the gang. Maybe he avoided a bad situation or maybe he will catch up someday. We will never know. I lost the record.

An acronym for BEHIND:

B   e yourself.

E   xpect God to

H   elp you.

I   n God find peace.

N   ever does He

D   esire for you to fail.

A GOOD SENSE OF DIRECTION

Once a year in Binghamton, New York, the local symphony orchestra would set up a huge float on the shore of the Susquehanna River and perform "Pops on the River." This was an event in our town that was well attended. One year when we attended with our children ages eight, seven, five, and two, we found a great spot down a trail to the riverbank. Mary Beth, our five-year-old daughter, somehow escaped our watchful eyes and became lost for over an hour. What a terrible experience for parents.

Mary Beth had met a police officer. He bought her an ice cream cone while we searched for her. Mary Beth wasn't afraid. She knew the policeman would help her find her parents again, and the ice cream was a great treat. She really had no idea of how serious her loss of direction could have been.

Most children don't get upset about loss of direction. They seem to have a childlike faith that they can find home again somehow. To children it is a game of "Hide-N-Seek." Speaking of "Hide-N-Seek," my two youngest daughters Debbie and Sarah scared me while we were at Wal-Mart one afternoon. They were only three and five years old at the time. They climbed under a rack of long dresses. They would not answer me when I frantically called their names. After what seemed to be eternity, I heard a quiet giggle and found those two rascals.

When my daughter Debbie was two years old, and I was eight-months pregnant with her sister Sarah, Debbie decided to go for a walk alone. Because I was unable to drive a car, Debbie and I walked everywhere together. She knew the way to the bus stop by heart. It was over two blocks away from our apartment. When we would wait for the bus, I would give her a ride on the mechanical carousel horse in front of the department store on Main Street.

The day Debbie disappeared, I was weeding my vegetable garden. She walked to Main Street and sat on the horse waiting for a ride. We called and searched for almost half an hour before we found her still sitting on the carousel horse. She wasn't worried at all. She knew where she was.

It's amazing how children even as young as two years old know direction. When my grandson Ryan was two years old, he demonstrated his good sense of direction. When his mother and he drove toward our home, Ryan pointed to the other side of the road and said, "No, that way see Papa." Papa is Ryan's Grandpa Harper who lived in a city about ten miles north of Grandpa and Grandma Mudge. Ryan had visited Papa the day before and remembered which way they had traveled to get there. Children learn direction fast. Children also have a childlike trust that they will always be safe.

Adults, on the other hand, become oppressed, depressed, and scared to move when they have turned in a wrong direction and feel lost. We need to become as little children and trust our heavenly Father for directions. Our Father will show us the way home just as I showed Debbie the way home from the carousel horse.

Our Father is just as concerned about us when we are lost. The only difference between me as Debbie's parent and God as our Father is that God waits for us to ask him for guidance. He will not force you to go home. You must want to go and you must ask him.

An acronym for LOST:

L   ost but
O   nly to yourself.
S   eek God's hand, and
T   rust him to lead you.

WHAT IS REALITY

hat is reality? It certainly isn't what television suggests to us. When I was approaching my final year of high school, I became very excited. I knew that I didn't have much longer till I could move out of my home of seventeen years and be on my own. I thought I would be happier. That was my vision of reality as a naïve, country girl at age seventeen.

Truth is I knew very little about reality until I moved out of my house. I rented a room forty-five miles away and shared the apartment with four other girls my age. The first week I was in that apartment, the other girls laughed at me. They were describing a pregnancy test. I made the mistake of asking what they were talking about. There were a lot of things I didn't know about yet. That apartment arrangement lasted only a month for me.

I tried two more times to live with other girls my age but didn't succeed in fitting in. I finally ended up renting a single room at the local YWCA. At the time, rent was only $16.50 a week. The room was very small. It only had a bed, a dresser, and a tiny closet. The bathroom with showers, the kitchen, and the television room were all community rooms.

There were many refrigerators in the kitchen. Each girl who paid rent had a key to the lock on a refrigerator.

Each refrigerator was used by five to eight girls for food storage. I didn't use the refrigerator much because girls kept on stealing my food. I decided to buy only canned goods and keep them in my room where they could not be stolen. I was going to college. I lived on money from grants and loans, so every penny counted.

The reality I discovered at the YWCA was that not everybody in the world is honest. Another reality I discovered was that not everybody was what I would call normal. One Thanksgiving I invited one of the girls from the YWCA to come and have dinner with my family because she had no family. At least that's what she told me. I hadn't known her very long. She was very appreciative for the meal. About two weeks later, I discovered my friend in her room passed out on the floor. She was high on drugs with an empty bottle of vodka beside her. It looked like a hurricane had gone through her room. She had thrown everything around before she fainted.

My friend got into trouble with the director for her actions. My friend got angry at me and threatened me bodily harm because she thought I had turned her into the director. Everyone on that floor had heard my friend's commotion and knew what had happened. Needless to say, we were no longer friends after that.

It was late at night, and most of the girls were out on the town or in bed. I couldn't sleep, so I decided to watch a late movie. I was the only person in the room until a very large woman in her thirties sat down on the opposite side of the sofa from me. She seemed to be high on drugs or drunk or both. Within a brief period of time she posed a question to me. I was still naïve, so it took a few minutes to realize what she was asking.

In shock I jumped up off that sofa and politely but

hurriedly said, "I go to bed alone." Needless to say, I stayed away from the community living room late at night after that.

The realities I found in the real world after leaving my home of seventeen years were shocking. I had been sheltered as a child growing up because of my disability. I had no idea what the real world was about.

Too often we think if we can just get out of a situation everything will be wine and roses. That reminds me of my very first poem I wrote at age nineteen.

It was a cold rainy night. I was still living at the YWCA. My room was on the fourth floor. The room had only one window. These words started coming to me as I looked out my window that night: "Wolves howl violently at my window as the days of wine and roses struggle within." I believe I had peace somewhere within, but so much reality of the evil of this world was coming into my life at one time that I felt like I was being attacked.

A short time after that I decided to go back to church. I had been away from church for almost two years. I thought it was not important in my life because I was busy with college and work. Months after I started going back to church, I wrote my second poem. "Alas, I see the dove pure and white. Its wings are wide open and soaring in flight. Come sail with me from sea to sea. Enjoy a life of peace, love, and tranquility."

Finally I had started seeing the good instead of the evil. I saw the dove instead of the wolves. The wolves were still there, but I chose to see the dove of peace.

Reality will always be there, but only you and I can choose whether to use our energy on welcoming in the dove or the wolves. This choice must be made daily. A good way to start and end the day is in prayer and praise and the reading of God's word. Another way to stay strong is to go to church and be an encouragement and a blessing to others.

An acronym for REALITY:

R   eal people
E   very day must
A   llow the dove of
L   ove and peace
I   n and
T   oss aside
Y   our wolves.

MOM'S TRIBUTE

Visions are for dreamers, Mom. I guess that means you're a dreamer. That's the major thing you taught me in my life.

From early childhood on, I can remember the wonderful, delicious smells that would flow from your kitchen. You are the best when it comes to cooking. I was always amazed at how you would have the food all ready at the same time. I always thought, as a child, that I would never be able to do that, but I have. Thanks, Mom.

When I would have epileptic convulsions all night long, you were always there. I saw you when I became conscience for brief periods between my convulsions. You were there watching and helping me, so I wouldn't bite my tongue or the sides of my mouth. I'm sure you were praying constantly. Thanks, Mom.

I could talk to you about anything. I even asked you questions about why a boy touched me in certain places and things like that. Most teenagers I know don't feel their mothers would understand them enough for them to open up to their moms. Thanks, Mom.

Being epileptic, I thank you for allowing me to take hikes in nature alone for hours. I loved picking strawberries or blackberries. I just loved to roam the vast woods and fields. You always trusted the Lord would protect me if I had a convulsion during my journeys. Thanks, Mom.

I enjoyed going to church with you every Sunday and going to special prayer services to pray for a healing of my epilepsy. I was totally delighted when I was old enough to sing in the church choir with you. It made me proud. Thanks, Mom.

I watched in excitement as you strived to achieve your vision. You had a vision of a lake on our property, and by the time you reached your midthirties, your vision was accomplished by the building of Glenn Lake. That took a belief and a determination to accomplish your vision. You taught me to try and try again. Thanks, Mom.

Mom, you taught me to have a vision and to dream. I thank you for that.

Love your daughter,
Barbara Ann